Bloody Brothers: America's First Serial Killers

By

Henry Lincoln Keel

DRP

DEEP READ PRESS
LAFAYETTE, TENNESSEE
deepreadpress@gmail.com

Text Copyright © 2021 by Henry Lincoln Keel

All Rights Reserved.

First Deep Read Press edition

Manufactured in the United States of America

ISBN: 978-1-954989-06-1
Edited by: Brenda LeCrone Seaberg
Cover Design by: Kim Gammon
Published by:
DEEP READ PRESS
Lafayette, Tennessee
www.deepreadpress.com

For my wife

Table of Contents

Introduction – 5
1. Their Early Days – 8
2. During the Revolution – 11
3. The New Land – 14
4. With the Renegades – 19
5. After Nickajack – 23
6. A Trail of Blood – 30
7. Escaping Justice – 40
8. Trying the Wrong People – 46
9. On to Cave-In-Rock – 51
10. The Spree Continues – 71
11. The end of Micajah Harpe – 88
12. The Harpe Women – 125
13. McBee's Avengers – 134
14. Rejoining Samuel Mason – 141
15. Wiley Harpe Testifies – 161
16. Another Escape – 191
17. The End of Wiley Harpe – 196
Afterword – 215
Bibliography – 217
About the Author – 220
Index – 221

Introduction

THIS is a true story, and it is as gruesome as any horror tale ever told.

Reputed brothers Micajah and Wiley Harpe hold the distinction of being America's first serial killers. At least, that is how leading criminologists and historians classify them. The Harpe brothers earned their title through displays of brutality seldom matched anywhere in the world, before or since.

To say the Harpe brothers were evil is a monumental understatement. They were so malicious that they repulsed other murderers and cutthroats, to the degree that they became outcasts even within the criminal community. Some criminal bands refused to have the Harpes as members, or if they did accept them, they threw them out quickly.

The Harpe brothers were thieves, to be sure, but profit was not their primary motivation. These two men humiliated and killed their victims for sheer pleasure. Before the authorities finally stopped them, the Harpes compiled a long list of victims – men, women, and children – in a very large area that included the present-day states of North Carolina, Tennessee, Kentucky, Illinois, Mississippi, Arkansas, and Louisiana.

This small volume details the Harpes' lives, their crimes, and their deaths. The author has not ventured to sensationalize any portion of the story. Of course, it is impossible to tell the story without adding uncomfortable, and even gory, details.

Everything in this volume is true and well-sourced. There was no need for embellishment, as the story is graphic enough on its own.

The author has tried, out of respect for the victims, to tell their stories just as they happened. There is no reason to make any broad judgments about these two men. Their evil deeds speak for them.

Occurring near the end of the eighteenth century, the criminal deeds of the Harpes across these several states and territories are virtually unequal in depravity and horror at any time in human history. While the records of the crimes committed by the Harpes are often sketchy, and, at times, contradictory, there is nothing to deny the statement that the Harpes were "the most brutal monsters of the human race."

The exact number of people the Harpes murdered during their killing spree is unknown. We are aware of at least 39 victims, while the actual number may have been more than 50, or possibly 100.

On the sparsely settled frontier, the isolated settlers often were not close enough together to see the smoke from their nearest neighbors' chimneys. Often, the pioneers simply disappeared without leaving a trace, and no one missed them. Most of these settlers despaired of the endless hard work with little, if any, profit, and climbed back over the mountains in search of less free but easier lives. Some even hoped to improve their prospects by moving ever deeper into the wilderness. Some of these absent settlers were also victims of murderers such as the Harpes brothers. As to how many of these unaccounted-for settlers the Harpes may have murdered is impossible to gauge, but the number may have been substantial.

While the Harpes sometimes robbed their victims for financial gain, that wasn't always true. The viciousness of their crimes, along with the fact that they murdered when they didn't have to, indicates that their motivation was more of a desire to satisfy their blood lust than to acquire wealth.

The primary purpose of this book, beyond telling the story of Micajah and Wiley Harpe, is to give readers the opportunity to think about serial killers in today's world, too. Sadly, people like the Harpes still walk among us today. Moreover, the obstacles that crime fighters face in stopping serial killers remain. Most of us have met people capable of being serial killers, and it is possible that our next-door neighbors are bloody brothers.

1. Their Early Days

THE Harpe brothers were born to Scottish parents in the North Carolina wilderness. Some sources contend that they were born in Scotland and moved to North Carolina, but there is no evidence to prove that.

Micajah "Big" Harpe was born between 1748 and 1767, with the earlier date being more likely. He died in August 1799. He was an intimidating figure, a massive man of at least six feet in height, and his frame was "robust." He stood very straight, with a large face and thick, jet-black curly hair. He also possessed extreme physical strength. Beyond that, he projected "an ill-looking, downcast countenance."

Micajah Harpe's size, coupled with his contempt for decency and his disregard for human life, made him a very, very dangerous man.

Wiley "Little", or "Redheaded", Harpe was born between 1750 and 1769. Again, the earlier date is most likely accurate. He died on February 8, 1804. He had a ruddy complexion and flaming red hair that was "not quite so curly as his brother's." Although he was the younger of the two men, Wiley looked very haggard and he appeared years older than Micajah. Like his brother, Wiley Harpe projected "a downcast countenance." Wiley Harpe, although considerably smaller than

Micajah, still had the ability to strike fear in those that crossed his path. He was also just as deadly as his older brother.

The facts surrounding the Harpes remain clouded, and the records are sparse. This has caused considerable disagreement as to the truth about their early lives. The best evidence shows that they were born in what is now Orange County, North Carolina. Although most accounts identify them as brothers, there is a belief among some historians that they were first cousins named Joshua and William Harper and that the two emigrated from Scotland in 1759 or 1760. The theory continues that their fathers were brothers named John and William Harper. However, there are holes in the "cousin" theory and this author prescribes to the more common view: that they were brothers.

The father of Micajah and Wiley Harpe held intense loyalty to the English king, serving in a Troy militia and fighting against his neighbors during the Regulator War between 1765 and 1771.

The Regulator War was an armed effort of North Carolina colonists to end the Royal interference in their affairs. Although the colonists failed, the Regulator War served as a precursor to the American Revolution.

After the Regulator War, their neighbors treated the members of the Harpe family as outcasts. Micajah and Wiley seethed with anger because of it. They promised to punish their neighbors for mistreating them.

The Harpe brothers did not intend to be poor dirt farmers for their entire lives. Instead, they had interest in becoming career men. Perhaps because of their general inhumanity and brutality, they decided they were suited to work as overseers of slaves on a big plantation. North Carolina did not offer them much opportunity, and in the springtime of 1775, the two men packed up their meager belongings and headed to Virginia to pursue their dreams. Evidently, the Harpe brothers failed to secure jobs as overseers in Virginia, and they drifted back to North Carolina.

2. During the Revolution

THE Harpes took sides during the American Revolution. As always seemed to be the case with them, they chose the wrong side. They supported the British Crown and took an active part during the war. Although the Harpes fought on the side of the British, they had no real loyalty for the motherland. Apparently, their interest was in taking retribution against their neighbors, burning farms, raping women, and pillaging.

Soon after the outbreak of the Revolution, the Harpes joined a pro-British "rape gang." These gangs preyed on Patriot civilians by raping, stealing, and murdering. They also burned and destroyed property. The rape gangs terrified the unprotected Patriot farmers, and disrupted food production that may have benefited Washington's Army.

The rape gangs didn't go unchallenged, however. The Patriots engaged them whenever possible. Once in North Carolina, Captain James Wood encountered the Harpe rape gang. The gang had already kidnapped, tortured, and raped three girls, and Wiley Harpe was raping a fourth when Wood arrived. Wood fired his rifle, wounding Wiley slightly. The scoundrel released the girl and ran away. Wiley Harpe survived the wound and promised to take revenge against Wood.

After their rape gang dissolved in 1780, the Harpes joined a band of military associators serving the British cause. The associators were not members of the British Army. The British did not provide them with uniforms, weapons, or pay. The associators survived by foraging, committing robbery, and looting battlefields. They differed from rape gangs only in the fact that they took part in regular military engagements.

Captain Wood's son, Frank, served as a militiaman with a group known as the "Overmountain Men." He was the older brother of Susan (aka Susanna) Wood. The Harpes later kidnapped Susan, and Micajah made her his wife.

Frank Wood witnessed the Harpe brothers taking part in the Battle of Kings Mountain in October 1780, on the side of the British. The Harpes were part of the militia group commanded by British Major Patrick Ferguson. During the three-hour battle, Frank Wood made a point of trying to kill Micajah Harpe, but his rifle shot went astray.

The Harpes later served under the command of Lieutenant Colonel Banastre Tarleton at the battles of Blackstock's Farm and Cowpens in January 1781.

At least one historian contends that the Harpes did not fight in the Revolutionary War, because they were too young. This historian contends that they were born in 1768 and 1770, respectively. He continues that it was the father (or fathers) of the Harpes that fought for the British. However, this historian does not attempt to explain how the boys could have sought to become slave overseers before either was a teenager, and before one was even ten years old.

3. The New Land

THE Harpes began their murder spree in east Tennessee. The area was sparsely settled and wild. The population was hardy, crude, resilient, and independent. The fresh, moist mountain air coursed through their lungs. They had ample game, fresh water, and an endless supply of fertile soil to claim, conquer, and cultivate.

These few thousand settlers also faced their share of hardships. The weather could be harsh, especially in the wintertime, and the storms and the flooding they brought wreaked havoc with the corn and other crops. If a farm family could not harvest all it needed, and wild game became scarce, hunger was likely, and starvation was possible. Cabin fires were common, and many a pioneer family lost all they owned because of too much soot in a chimney flue or an untimely spark from a fireplace.

Those trying to tame the land also faced physical danger. There were more bears in Tennessee than there were people, and large cats were always on the prowl. There were also poisonous snakes almost everywhere. Since doctors were few and of poor quality, and the pioneers could not treat themselves, they were likely not to survive. Beyond that, large herds of buffalo roamed the area, and deadly stampedes were more common than one might suppose.

The settlers were also accustomed to atrocities. Sometimes they committed the atrocities against the Native population; sometimes they suffered by atrocities from the Natives. Atrocities were an unpleasant fact that most of the settlers accepted as something they just had to deal with, like thunderstorms and droughts. Yet, despite the hardships, if one had a strong back, a little good luck with the weather, and a lot of courage, it was possible to carve out a decent living in the lush, green wilderness.

Driven by the same impulses that caused Europeans to flow across the Atlantic Ocean to North America two centuries before, thousands of Americans streamed across the mountains and into the vast, empty land west of the Appalachian Mountains and east of the Mississippi River. Slowly, this wilderness began to fill up with souls looking for a better life.

The new settlers were Americans in the truest sense. As a rule, they were not sophisticated or well-educated, but they were proud, brave, and willing to face almost any challenge to make their own way. At least, that described most of the settlers that braved the obstacles associated with the move inland from the edge of the Atlantic Ocean.

The majority of those moving across the mountains into the wilderness were honest, hardworking folk. They wanted nothing more than the opportunity to earn a living on their own without a greedy landlord bearing down on them constantly.

Sadly, other types moved west as well. A small minority of the new settlers did not share the pioneer spirit or have any desire to build a life through industrious effort. Some of these settlers were fugitives from justice. They had migrated to the wilderness as a way to avoid those wishing to jail them. For these people, the wild and open frontier offered them a place to hide, and perhaps, a base of operation from which to continue their criminal careers.

The honest pioneers usually had no problem dealing with criminals. They saw their share of outlaws and dealt with them harshly. However, the brutal, often senseless, and always unprovoked murders committed by the Harpe brothers repulsed the hardy pioneer folk and gripped them with horror.

If there had been anything like the wanton killings perpetrated by the Harpes before in North America, no one was aware of it. Native Americans launched their attacks with a purpose in mind. There was not much reason behind the slaughter committed by the Harpes, beyond the perverse pleasure they took from killing.

The minds of serial killers are still a mystery to us in the 21st Century, and the motivations of the Harpes certainly baffled the citizens in the 18th Century. They were like some incurable virus that ravished the countryside and struck its victims at random. There was no tried and true method for dealing with the menace because it was a new malady. No community had ever dealt with serial killers before.

From losing children at childbirth, to cabin fires, to epidemics of yellow fever and other diseases, to war, to animal attacks, to dealing with murderers, no Americans had witnessed more death than the backwoods pioneers had. Yet, the murder spree of the Harpes shook the people of this "New West" like nothing before. The crimes these men committed set the whole county ablaze with fear and loathing. The good folk knew the evil was out there somewhere and that it might blow over them like a foul wind at any time. Surely, the poor frightened people thought, the Devil had total control of the territory the Harpes operated. As one observer put it:

"Neither avarice nor want nor any of the usual inducements to the commission of crime, seemed to govern their conduct. A savage thirst for blood – a deep-rooted enmity against human nature, could alone be discovered in their actions . . . Plunder was not their object; they took only what would have been freely given them, and no more than what was necessary to supply the immediate wants of nature ; they destroyed without having suffered injury, and without the prospect of benefit . . . Mounted on fine horses they plunged into the forest, eluded pursuit by frequently changing their course, and appeared unexpectedly to perpetrate new horrors, at points distant from those where they were supposed to lurk."

The Harpes practiced "such disgusting . . . human depravity and barbarism" and a "total disregard of the morals of the community."

"However it may be regretted that such monsters as the Harpes ever should have existed to disgrace humanity, yet it is an incontrovertible fact."

Shortly before he died, Micajah Harpe said he committed so many murders because many people had treated him badly and he had become "disgusted with all mankind."

Some attributed a racist reason for the Harpes acts. A myth arose that "their tawny appearance and dark curly hair betrayed a tinge of African blood coursing through their veins." The ridiculous theory assumed that persons of African decent are more likely to commit crimes, such as the savage and terrible murders committed by the Harpes, than others were. Not only is that untrue, but there is no evidence to indicate that the Harpes were related to anyone of African heritage. In fact, Wiley Harpe's hair was not dark – it was red.

4. With the Renegades

THE Harpes were never loyalists in the true sense of the word. They engaged in the war to punish their North Carolina neighbors for abusing them. Besides that, they took great pleasure in pillaging and murdering, especially if their victims could not fight back. They soon tired of the restrictions – as few as they were – that the British placed on them, and they decided to make their way across the mountains where they could live their lives unfettered and uncivilized.

Wiley Harpe was intent on making good his promise to take vengeance on Captain Wood, and before they departed over the mountains, he and Micajah Harpe kidnapped Wood's daughter, Susan, and another girl named Maria Davidson (aka Betsey, or Betsy, or Betty Wood Roberts). The two girls may have been sisters.

The Harpes declared the girls were their wives, but eventually Micajah Harpe took sole possession of both, and each of them bore him children. While Micajah Harpe claimed both women as his wives, the truth is that he had the same indifference towards matrimony as he did for all other conventions. Moreover, even though Wiley Harpe conceded the women to his older brother, he, too, brutalized and forced the girls into intercourse with him.

The Harpes, their brutalized "wives", and four other men crossed the Smokey Mountains into the land that would become Tennessee. It seems that Moses Doss, one of those accompanying the Harpes, expressed concern for the battered females. Micajah Harpe repaid the concern Doss displayed by murdering him and leaving his corpse on the trail for the buzzards.

In 1781, they joined and lived among the renegade Chickamauga Cherokee. They didn't abandon their violent ways, however. On April 2, the Harpes joined a war party of 400 Chickamauga Cherokee, led by Chief Dragging Canoe, against the Patriot frontier settlement of Bluff Station at Fort Nashborough (present-day Nashville) in the Battle of the Bluffs. The settlers withstood the assault and repelled Dragging Canoe's force.

On August 19, 1782, the Harpes were members of a Chickamauga Cherokee war party that traveled to Kentucky. Backed by the British, they defeated an army of Patriot pioneers led by Daniel Boone at the Battle of Blue Licks.

The Harpes took part in other skirmishes among their Chickamauga Cherokee friends and Patriots, but none of the battles affected the outcome of the Revolution.

The Harpes spent a dozen or so years with the Chickamauga Cherokee at a village southwest of present-day Chattanooga called Nickajack. The Harpes found Nickajack a convenient base for their criminal enterprise. They also continued to exhibit inhuman brutality. An unconfirmed story gained currency that Micajah Harpe's two wives each gave birth to two children during their stay at Nickajack, and that he murdered the infants.

Their own tribes had ostracized the renegade Chickamauga Cherokees, and they committed atrocities against Natives as well as the white settlers living near them. This suited the Harpes fine. They enjoyed terrorizing and murdering others, regardless of skin color. The Harpes were students of barbarity and they learned a great deal about the science of cruelty from the renegades, just as they had from the Troy rape gang during the war.

The Harpes also knew how to stay safe from attack. They were forever on guard, and they kept their tomahawks and knives with them even when they slept. They never left camp unarmed, and they made even their allies know that they would kill anyone that crossed them or threatened them in any way. Their renegade allies marveled at the fact that the Harpes preferred living like wild beasts and took satisfaction from shedding blood pointlessly.

The Harpe men and their women wore leather hunting shirts and moccasins made from the hides of the wild animals they killed, but unlike the renegades, the Harpes didn't bother to tan the hides they used for clothing. The Harpes didn't don hats except during the coldest days, and their hats were merely animal hides sewn together with deerskin strings.

Another technique the Harpes learned was the use of false identities. They employed aliases whenever meeting new people and they claimed to have various vocations, from farmers, to preachers, to horse traders. Their deceptions usually succeeded.

Although the new American government considered anyone aiding renegades criminal outlaws, the Harpes apparently maintained friendly contacts with some of the white settlers near Nickajack. In September 1794, the Americans felt it was time to use force against the residents of Nickajack and planned a major military assault there. The Harpes learned of the attack before it happened and they fled just ahead of the American militiamen that slaughtered the villagers and wiped out Nickajack.

5. After Nickajack

THE Harpe brothers had long before decided that honest work did not suit them, and they embarked upon criminal careers. Since lawmen were sparse west of the Appalachians, the Harpes found easy pickings among the honest frontier settlers. They robbed and killed with impunity for an extended period. Little things, such as the destruction of their Nickajack homes of a dozen years, did not convince them to reform.

After fleeing Nickajack, the Harpes and their women made camp a few miles from the burned out village. They remained there for about nine months. While at their camp, the men continued to rob the residents in the area.

The Harpes next drifted northeast to Powell's Valley, near Knoxville, where they continued their outlaw ways. Instead of earning an honest living from the fertile soil offered them by the valley, they found it easier to steal food, supplies, and what little money the settlers may have had. Law enforcement in the area was virtually nonexistent, and the Harpes were so ferocious that their crimes went unchallenged.

There are only a couple of known instances where the Harpes let a person go once he was in their clutches. Soon after relocating to the Knoxville area, the two criminals came across a young man who was traveling through the wilderness alone. The man, William Lambuth, was a Methodist minister. Lambuth was armed, but the Harpes surprised him and took his gun. They intended to murder Lambuth, but they left him alive and uninjured, while they pilfered through his belongings.

The Harpes were expert highwaymen and knew that travelers often hid paper currency between the pages of books. They grabbed Lambuth's Bible from him and started fanning through it looking for cash. To his surprise, on the very first page of the old Bible, Micajah Harpe read the names "William Lambuth" and "George Washington." General Washington had just completed his tenure as President of the United States, but Micajah Harpe knew him more as a great General than as a political figure. The massive outlaw held the Bible up and pointed to Washington's name. Then he said to Wiley in a loud voice, "That is a brave and good man, but a mighty rebel against the King."

The items they found among Lambuth's belongings convinced them that he was indeed a minister and a brave man. Because of this, not only did they spare his life, but they also returned the preacher's Bible, his gun, the little money he had, and his horse. In fact, all they wanted from the youthful man of the cloth was his recognition of them as the persons that had robbed him. As they were riding away, they shouted loud enough to make him remember, "We are the Harpes."

Knoxville was a young, rambunctious town when the Harpes relocated near it. There was more than enough evidence to prove Knoxville was an outpost of many crude, criminal types.

James Weir, writing about Knoxville during the period that the Harpes came to the area, related that the "houses are irregular and interspersed." He continued that when he visited Knoxville was "County Court day" and that the "town was confused with a promiscuous throng of every denomination. Some talked, some sang, and mostly all did profanely swear." Weir expressed his shock at hearing "the horrid oaths and dreadful indignities offered to the Supreme Governor of the Universe, who with one frown is able to shake them into non-existence."

Weir added that he was aghast that Knoxville did not to appear to adhere to the Blue Laws enforced east of the mountains. He felt repulsed that city leaders in Knoxville permitted townsfolk to participate in "dancing, singing, and playing of cards, etc.", even on Sundays.

Finally, Weir agreed with a citizen of Knoxville that "the Devil is grown so old that it renders him incapable of traveling and that he has taken up in Knoxville and there hopes to spend the remaining part of his days in tranquility, as he believes he is among his friends." If the Devil had retired to Knoxville, he certainly had friends in the brothers Harpe.

Allies of Satan or not, the Harpes moved near Knoxville because it offered them a larger quantity of victims than did the wilderness from which they came. They moved onto a tract of cleared land adjacent to Beaver Creek, about eight miles to the west of Knoxville. There, they gave the appearance of being typical pioneers. They constructed a crude log cabin, a corral for their horses, and even planted a few crops.

The Harpes seemed so normal and upright that they quickly gained the acceptance of their neighbors. Within weeks, Wiley Harpe romanced Sarah (better known as Sally) Rice, and she fell in love with him. She was the daughter of John Rice, a preacher that lived about four miles north of the Harpe shack. Wiley Harpe fooled Reverend Rice to the degree that he consented to allow his bedazzled daughter to wed the outlaw.

Although the Harpes were doing a good job of hiding their true natures, they did not change their wicked behavior. On one of their first trips to the town of Knoxville, they brought with them a beautiful three year old mare and offered to run her in a stakes race. The Harpes' steed was so obviously superior to any other horse in Knoxville that no one took the Harpes up on their offer for a race.

However, a man named Aycoff so prized the animal that he paid the Harpes a good price for her. Aycoff loved the mare and kept her until about 1820. Around two decades after Aycoff bought the horse, a man from Georgia passing through Knoxville saw the animal and recognized her as the filly stolen from him years before.

The Harpes could not keep up their pretense of honesty indefinitely. Their true nature had to bleed through eventually. It was sooner, rather than later. Most of the farmers in the outlying area made very few trips into town. There was simply too much time-consuming work for them to waste time on making unnecessary trips to Knoxville. Contrary to their neighbors, the Harpes made an increasing number of treks into the city. As unusual as their constant trips into town were, other things aroused suspicion in the community, too. Every time the Harpes came to town, they had more freshly butchered pork and mutton than the time before. They sold the meat to respected merchant John Miller, and Harpe hams became well known throughout the city.

People notice things, though, and it seemed strange to Miller and others that the Harpes had so much meat to sell when it was impossible for them to raise that many animals in such a short period. They also didn't have the funds to purchase that much livestock from their neighbors. Miller soon became convinced that they were stealing hogs and sheep, and he stopped buying from the Harpes.

The Harpes did other things that lowered their reputations among the citizens of Knoxville. On their numerous trips to town, they drank heavily, gambled constantly, and created violent disturbances. As crude as they were themselves, those living in Knoxville came to feel that the Harpes were pests. They wanted to see the pair gone. As time went on, their opinions sank even lower, and they viewed the Harpes as miscreants whose dishonesty and meanness had no limit.

Soon after the Harpes arrived in the Knoxville area, houses, barns, and stables went up in flames with no apparent cause or motive. The citizens attributed the crimes to malicious mischief. At first, there were no suspects, but the behavior of the Harpes led townsfolk to think that the Harpes were likely the culprits. There was no solid evidence against the Harpes, and the citizens could do nothing against them. With no other alternative, they waited for the two rascals to give themselves away.

A little while after the Harpes came under suspicion, Edward Tiel found several of his best horses missing. Tiel, who lived only about a mile from Knoxville, decided without evidence that the Harpes were guilty, and he was determined to do something about it. Tiel gathered a posse and went to the Harpe cabin, but they were not there. Perhaps someone tipped them off that a posse was on its way, but whether or not that was true, the Harpes abandoned their shack just before Tiel and his men arrived.

Still searching for positive proof against outlaws, the investigators found evidence that a large number of horses had earlier been tied to trees near the Harpe residence. This was enough for Tiel and his men to continue their pursuit.

The Harpes were old hands at avoiding pursuers, and they were certain that they could avoid capture from the amateurs chasing them. Thus, they did nothing to hide their tracks and left an easy trail for the Tiel posse to follow.

Tiel and his men followed the Harpes westerly across the Clinch River and into the Cumberland Mountains. Surprising their quarry as they camped alone, Tiel and his men captured the horse thieves without a struggle. The Harpe brothers had Tiel's horses in their possession, and they made no protest of their innocence. In fact, the Harpes seemed willing to follow all the instructions their captors gave them.

Having succeeded in their quest, Tiel and his men began transporting the felons back to Knoxville for trial. Perhaps because the horse thieves had behaved so gentlemanly towards the posse, Tiel and his men were lax in guarding their prisoners. About five miles northeast of Knoxville, the Harpes bolted and got away from the posse. Tiel and his men began chasing after the escapees but lost track of them, deciding to return home. Tiel reasoned the mission was a success even if he didn't bring the Harpes to justice. After all, he had regained his valuable livestock and the outlaws were gone.

6. A Trail of Blood

THE Harpes were now on the run. But they were not very concerned about a posse catching them. As is usual for their ilk, they believed they were smarter than were their pursuers. In fact, they seemed to take a perverse pleasure in justice.

Evidently, the Harpes felt they were safe enough to have a little of their brand of "fun" before they departed the Knoxville area. The same night that they escaped the Tiel posse, they rode a few miles west of Knoxville to an inn referred to as "Hughes' Rowdy Groggery." Hughes, two of his brothers-in-law named Metcalf, and a man from Jefferson County, Tennessee, named Johnson, were there. The Rowdy Groggery was a rough place, and the Harpes had been there before. Some of those present at the inn recognized the Harpes as the bandits rushed through the door.

No one saw Johnson alive after that night. A few days later, Johnson's mutilated body appeared floating in the Holstein River. The sight was horrible. The murderers had killed Johnson, urinated upon his corpse, and then mutilated his body by ripping open its chest cavity and filling it with rocks to weigh it down. Then they dumped their victim into the water. Johnson's body sank, but after a while, the rocks became displaced and the fast-decaying corpse floated to the surface.

This grotesque signature method of body disposal served as something of a calling card for the Harpes. If they settled upon it as a means to strike fear in possible opponents, they succeeded. The sheer brutality of their technique unnerved many of their pursuers.

After the discovery of Johnson's body, Hughes and the Metcalf men came forward and told authorities about the events on the last night of Johnson's life. Hughes and the others stated that, in their opinion, the Harpes, who were still fugitives, committed the crime.

The authorities did not automatically accept the story Hughes and his in-laws gave them. Hughes was not a man of high moral standing, and no witness other than the three put the Harpes at the groggery on the night Johnson disappeared. In fact, the common belief was that the Harpes had fled the area as soon as they escaped from Tiel's posse. Instead of sending out a party in search of the Harpes, the authorities arrested Hughes and the Metcalf brothers for killing Johnson and cast them in jail.

There was no evidence that the accused parties had killed Johnson, and a jury acquitted them. The locals did not approve of the acquittal and promised to exact the justice that the court refused to order. The Metcalf brothers, fearing for their lives, abandoned all and fled the area immediately. Hughes refused to be intimated – at least, at first. He returned home, intent upon resuming his business as if nothing had happened. He should have taken the threats more seriously. A group of "regulators" soon appeared at the Rowdy Groggery, bound him, beat him with a horsewhip, tore down his home, and drove him away from East Tennessee.

As stated earlier, the Harpes employed their signature method of body disposal on several other occasions, and there is no doubt that they murdered Johnson. Of course, the charges against Hughes and the Metcalf brothers were wrong – as was the abuse visited upon Hughes. If the Harpes ever learned of the fate of their accusers, it likely amused them to no end.

The Johnson slaying was not the first act of homicide the Harpes committed, but it was the first murder they committed during the spree that made them the most infamous murderers of their age – perhaps of any age. Before the Johnson murder, the Harpes were mainly ruffians, low-level thieves, and arsonists. Now they began on a path "so bold that it not only terrified the citizens of Tennessee and Kentucky, but also alarmed settlers in many other sections of the Middle West."

After killing Johnson, the spree killers hastened to western Virginia, where they met their three women near Cumberland Gap. From there, they entered Kentucky in December 1798. Kentucky, which had gained statehood only in 1792, had a bad reputation. It had earned the nickname of "dark and bloody ground," but over the next year, the Harpes brought more darkness and spilled more blood in the Bluegrass State than anyone could have possibly imagined.

The Harpes were likely attracted to Kentucky because while it had a population of about 200,000, the western and southern portions of the state, except along the major waterways, were wilderness. There, the mighty buffalo grazed, and the powerful bear foraged in numbers greater than the human population.

Travel along the famous Wilderness Road was easy enough for the Harpes, and they strayed away from it only when they were avoiding posses or other trackers. They often had pursuers because they never attempted to restrain their murderous passions. When they felt like shedding blood, they shed blood. Oddly, the Harpe party never seemed to hurry unless hotly chased. The Harpe men rode along slowly on horseback while their women followed a few feet behind them on foot.

The first murder the Harpes committed in Kentucky took place near the Cumberland River in present-day Knox County. They came across and killed a peddler named Peyton, taking his horse and many of the goods he was carrying. The Peyton murder was so vicious that it drew more attention than some of the other Harpe murders.

The Harpes moved along the Wilderness Road, toward Crab Orchard and Stanford in Lincoln County, where they came upon two men from Maryland going in the same direction. The two men, named Bates and Paca, agreed to move along with the Harpes and make camp with them as soon as they agreed upon a suitable spot. There were several locations agreeable to the men from Maryland, but the Harpes refused to stop. They said they wanted to find a more desirable camping site.

Dusk came and the group continued to move along. In the poor light, Micajah Harpe moved up behind Bates, and Wiley Harpe came close behind Paca. The women walked about thirty feet behind the men and never made a sound as the Harpes raised their weapons and fired. Both victims fell to the ground. Bates died instantly. Paca suffered a severe wound, but he struggled, trying to get to his feet. Micajah Harpe would have none of it. He ran up to Paca and stopped him from rising by "splitting open his head with the tomahawk he carried in his belt."

After killing Bates and Paca, the Harpes took any of their clothing that the brothers could use, along with all the gold, silver, and coins that their victims were carrying. Then they continued along the Wilderness Road as if nothing had happened.

Stephen Langford came from a wealthy family in Mecklenburg County, Virginia. In the autumn of 1798, the young man wanted thrills and adventure, and he decided to feed his wanderlust by traveling down Boone's Trace into Kentucky. Langford had relatives at Crab Orchard, Kentucky, and he intended to visit them. He also thought he might relocate there, or perhaps in Frankfort, Kentucky.

Langford and his traveling companion, David Irby, set out from Pittsylvania County Virginia and headed toward Kentucky. The two traveled for five days, sharing expenses as they went. Langford noted every transaction in his pocket book. Before they crossed English's Ferry in Wythe County, Virginia, Irby purchased half a bushel of oats for their horses, plus a quantity of cheese for the two men to eat, and Langford noted it in his pocket book.

Langford and Irby continued together on the trail from Virginia, to the Cumberland Gap, into northeastern Tennessee, before reaching Kentucky. The two men then separated and agreed to meet at Frankfort, Kentucky, later.

The further west one traveled, the more dangerous the wilderness became. Suffering from the recklessness of youth, Langford rode across the frontier alone. He wasn't concerned about highwaymen waylaying him along the trail. He was so full of a sense of adventure that he had no room for caution.

On the chilly evening of December 12, 1798, not far from Crab Orchard, Langford stopped at a public house near the Big Rockcastle River. The public house, owned by John Farris, Sr., sat at the crossroads of nowhere, but it was a popular place. Travelers usually didn't like to proceed deeper into the Kentucky wilderness alone. They would stop and wait for other travelers to arrive, wanting the safety groups offered. Langford had no fear of traveling by himself, and he did not want to delay his trip waiting for other travelers who might – or might not – wander past. He was determined to rest a bit and then go on his way.

As the two talked, Farris realized he had known the Langford family in Virginia. The two hit it off, and Langford spent the night at the Farris public house.

The next morning Langford was up early. He intended to have a large, hot breakfast and then continue his journey. Langford was in a jovial mood.

While Langford patiently waited for Jane Farris, the daughter-in-law of John Farris, to finish preparing breakfast, the Harpe brothers and their women came up tentatively to the door of the public house and asked to come inside just long enough to warm themselves. Farris welcomed them out of the cold.

The Harpes were a haggard lot. They were filthy, even for people who had been on the Wilderness Road for days. They didn't have much in the way of material possessions either. The horses the Harpe men rode were poor specimens, and the poor animals hadn't eaten anything in days except what grass they could graze on along the frozen trail. There were a few bags hanging across the malnourished horses, and other than those and the two rifles they carried, the Harpe party had nothing else.

When Langford saw the Harpes, he felt pity for them immediately. The Harpes put on an air of ferociousness, but Langford, a poor judge of character, attributed that to their obvious hunger. He didn't consider for a moment that these poor creatures could be outlaws.

Langford struck up a conversation with the men and discovered they were, like him, strangers to the area. They didn't talk much, and were reluctant to divulge their intended destination. The young man didn't press them; he figured it was none of his business.

While Langford and the Harpes talked, Jane Farris placed breakfast on the long wooden table in the large dimly lit, one-room building, and bid everyone to sit and eat. Of course, the food wasn't offered free of charge and the Harpes declined to sit down, saying they had no currency to spend. The generous Langford chuckled and invited the Harpes and their women to have a meal at his expense. His five guests, thinking nothing of the cost to Langford, ate like ravenous animals.

After everyone devoured breakfast, Langford asked for the bill and in the act of paying, he pulled a handful of silver coins from his pocket. The sight of the money caused a reaction from the Harpe men, who suddenly became much friendlier. One of them asked if Langford wanted to travel with them. The impetuous young man agreed. They didn't depart right away, however.

After breakfast, Langford and the Harpes "appeared cheerful with one another." Langford "seemed somewhat intoxicated." He had a small glass bottle that he filled with whiskey at the public house on the previous evening, and he had evidently been drinking all morning.

As was the custom of the time, Langford wore leggings, and he had torn one of them in the brush during his long ride. Susan Harpe offered to darn it for him, but she said she only had white thread. Langford, not caring about the thread color, let her sew them for him.

Just before they departed, Langford and the Harpe men had an argument of some sort, and Langford became embarrassed. He apologized to Jane Farris and told her "in the presence of all, that he would not offend her for all in his saddle bags which was worth five hundred pounds."

Despite the fact that John Farris cautioned Langford not to travel with the obviously disreputable Harpes, the young man left with them. No one, except his killers, ever saw Langford alive again.

On December 14, just one day after the Harpes and Langford took up company together, drovers were pushing a herd of cattle to Virginia. The cowpunchers traveled on the same road as the villains and their prey. A few miles from Rockcastle River, the cattle "took fright, and, quitting the road, rushed down a hill into the woods."

While the cattlemen were gathering up their strays, they found the body of a man hidden behind a log. Inspecting the body, they found it "exhibited marks of violence." The drovers had no doubt that the dead man was the victim of foul play. They loaded the body into a wagon intending to report the crime and get the poor soul a proper burial. The cattlemen carried the body to the nearest public place – the Farris house where the Harpes had breakfasted a few days before.

Langford's last known companions were the "squalid and miserable" Harpes, and they fell under immediate suspicion. Law enforcement had not yet found the murdered Maryland travelers and the peddler, but one murder conviction would be enough to end their terrible spree.

David Irby heard rumors that highwaymen murdered his friend Thomas Langford, and Irby left immediately for the scene where the deed took place. When he arrived at the public house, Irby learned from John Farris that Abraham Anthony had already buried the murdered man, believed to be Thomas Langford. Irby wanted to know if the dead man was Langford, and Farris seemed uncertain.

The Logan County, Kentucky, coroner held an inconclusive inquest ,and then agreed to allow Farris and Irby to exhume the body. They, along with Anthony, "raised him and inspected him."

When the men removed the body from the ground, Irby identified it as his good friend, Thomas Langford, immediately. John Farris remained unconvinced until he noticed that the corpse was missing a tooth. Farris remembered that when he met Langford, he had noticed that the young man was missing a tooth in the same location as the corpse. The missing tooth convinced Farris that the dead man was Stephen Langford.

7. Escaping Justice

CAPTAIN Joseph Ballenger was a prominent merchant and militia leader from the town of Stanford in Lincoln County, Kentucky. On either December 19 or 20, 1798, Ballenger received a request from Kentucky Attorney General John Blair to put together and lead a posse in pursuit of the Harpes. Ballenger agreed to do so, and he promised to keep up the chase until he caught them.

After murdering Langford, the Harpes continued to Crab Orchard, then turned northwest along Frankfort Road toward Stanford. Once they arrived in Stanford, they turned back toward the west and headed deeper into the western Kentucky wilderness.

The Harpes believed they had hidden the corpse of their breakfast benefactor well enough that no one would find him for many days, if at all. That being the case, they had ambled along slowly, without much concern that anyone might be on their trail. When the Harpes stopped to rest, they didn't bother to post one of the women as a guard.

On Christmas Day, 1798, Ballenger's posse found the Harpes near a place then called Carpenter's Station. Carpenter's Station was near Hustonville, about eight miles southwest of Stanford. Ballenger came upon the complacent Harpes sitting on a log and ordered his men to rush them. The surprised outlaws realized they were outgunned and that they could not get to their horses to escape, so they surrendered without resistance.

After they had the Harpes brothers subdued, Captain Ballenger and his men searched the suspects. According to Ballenger, his inspection proved the Harpes possessed several items, shown later to belong to Langford. These included a pocket book with the name of Thomas Langford, along with a great coat, gray coating cloth, short coat with pieces of broken glass in one of the pockets, "mixed colored" long coat, pair of breeches, shaving glass, whip, pair of wrappers, horse, Free Mason's apron, and other unspecified items. The physical evidence convinced Ballenger and his men beyond any doubt that the Harpes were the murders.

The posse did not find Langford's money. He had a pocket full of silver coins, and if the young man was telling the truth, he had another £500 in his saddlebags. The Harpes could not have spent such a large amount in the short period they were on the run, so it was presumed that they must have hidden it on the trail for later use. Rumors arose that they used the money to purchase their freedom, but no one ever proved it.

Ballenger and his band transported their five prisoners to Stanford, a town of less than 200, then lodged them in the Logan County jail. The jail was a log cabin consisting of two twelve-foot square cells. The Harpe men stayed in one cell and the women in another. Satisfied that they had done their duty, the posse broke up, its members going home to wait on the court to render justice upon the Harpes.

On January 4, 1799, a mere ten days after they went to jail, the Harpes had a hearing before the three judges of the Lincoln County Court of Quarter Sessions, Hugh Logan, William Montgomery, and Nathan Huston. The charge against them was "feloniously and of their malice aforethought murdering and robbing a certain Thomas Langford on Wednesday the 12th day of December 1798 on the road leading from Kentucky to Virginia through the Wilderness."

Of course, the proceeding was a major event and the little county swelled with those wishing to witness the notorious Harpes and their women. The consensus was that soon the county Sheriff would hang the Harpe men – and maybe the women, too.

The hearing took place in the Logan County Courthouse. The log courthouse was T-shaped, thirty feet long and twenty feet wide, with a small jury room on each side. Spectators overfilled the courthouse during the hearing.

The accused identified themselves as Micajah Roberts [Micajah Harpe], Wiley Roberts [Wiley Harpe], Susanna Roberts [Susan Harpe], Sally Roberts [Sally Harpe], and Elizabeth Walker [Betsey Harpe]. Exactly why Betsey Harpe, one of the women Micajah Harpe claimed as a wife, did not give her name as Roberts is uncertain. She may have been trying to save Micajah Harpe from a bigamy charge; she may have been trying to separate herself from the other defendants; or it may have been for some other reason. We will likely never know her motivation.

Oddly, all three of the Harpe women were pregnant and all three delivered babies while incarcerated.

All five defendants entered pleas of "Not Guilty," and they had the opportunity to speak in their own defense. But they said nothing to prove their innocence.

Thomas Todd, the prosecuting attorney, called five witnesses to testify against the Harpes. The first was Captain Ballenger. Ballenger testified to chasing and capturing the Harpes, and to the items belonging to Langford that he found during the search.

David Irby took the stand next. His testimony that the pocket book found on the Harpes belonged to Langford was telling.

John Farris Sr. testified next. He related what happened at his public house, including that Langford and the Harpes left together.

Jane Farris also testified. She and her husband, William Farris, also lived at the public house, and she identified various items found in the possession of the Harpes as belonging to Langford.

Thomas Welsh was one of the posse members, and his testimony mirrored that of Captain Ballenger.

After hearing the Harpes weakly defend themselves, the judges rendered their decision that the Harpes "ought to be tried for the murder [of Langford] before the Judges of the

District Court holden for the Danville District at the next April Term, and it is ordered that they be remanded to jail."

On January 5, Lincoln County Sheriff Joseph Welsh and seven guards escorted the five people ten miles through the incessant forest from Stanford to the Danville jail, turning them over to "Jailer of the District of Danville," John Biegler.

Danville had a population of a little more than 200, but it was one of the more important Kentucky towns. The Danville courthouse was about fifteen years old, and consisted of "a log house large enough for a court room in one end, and two jury rooms in the other end on the same floor . . . and a prison of hewed or sawed logs at least nine inches thick."

Micajah Harpe continued to be arrogant during his incarceration. He offered to fistfight the two best men in Kentucky at once, provided the jailer would release him if he won, and if he failed, he would abide by the judgment of the court. Of course, no fight ever took place. Micajah Harpe never intended to wait for the court to convict and hang him. He and his brother planned to take flight as soon as the opportunity arose.

Jailer Biegler apparently made some effort to keep the Harpes from escaping. On January 20, he purchased "Two horse locks to chain the men's feet to the ground." Then, on February 13, in order to secure the jail better, he bought "one lock for front jail door." Two weeks after that, Biegler purchased three pounds of nails "for the use of the jail." Furthermore, the jailer employed four men, two per shift, to guard the prisoners.

Despite all the efforts to keep them in custody, the Harpes escaped on March 16, leaving their women and newborn infants in custody. Evidently, the Harpes made a hole in the wall of the jail and broke through it. On March 19, the jailer procured materials for "Mending the wall in jail where the prisoners escaped." According to sources, the Harpes also took two of the guards' rifles when they left. No one ever confirmed if they took the guns during a scuffle or if the guards left the weapons unattended.

Rumors soon emerged that jailer Biegler conspired to aid the escape of the Harpes. A historian later wrote "the jailer, soon after their escape, resigned his office, left the jail, bought a farm and settled himself in the country where he very shortly became wealthy – no one ever knew with certainty by what means, but the general suspicion was that he had acquired his wealth by receiving a large bribe from the Harpes to permit them to escape."

It is unknown if the Harpes paid off John Biegler. They certainly would have offered him anything to let them go, possibly even the hidden fortune they had stolen from Thomas Langford. However, no one ever produced enough evidence against Biegler to charge him with the illicit release of the Harpes.

8. Trying the Wrong People

UNABLE to try the despicable Harpe men, the court proceeded to do the next best thing and put the women on trial. The poor wretches had already suffered greatly. They, all of them pregnant, spent the cold, hard Kentucky winter in the freezing jail awaiting trial for murder. Beyond that, their "husbands" thought so little of them that they abandoned them to stand trial for the crimes the men committed.

The Harpe women were a hardy lot. Their uncaring men had forced them to walk through the wilderness even late into their pregnancies. Then, they had the indignity of delivering their children while in jail.

On February 7, 1799, Betsey Harpe delivered a son. Lincoln County paid a midwife 21 shillings to aid in the delivery. The county also provided the woman with Hyson tea, sugar, and ginger to help her regain her strength after giving birth.

On March 6, Susan Harpe gave birth to a daughter. She received similar benefits as Betsey, but the county only paid her midwife 18 shillings.

Finally, on April 8, the last of the Harpe women, Sally, delivered her child – a little girl. Her delivery must have been difficult because the county spent 6 shillings on whiskey for her use during the birth.

The trial of the three women began on Monday, April 15, 1799 in the Danville District Court. The presiding officials were Judges James G. Hunter and Samuel McDowell. McDowell served in the absence of Judge Stephen Ormsby. All three women stood accused of the murder of Thomas Langford.

The jailer brought Susan Harpe, "spinster of Lincoln County," before the judges, and she entered a "not guilty" plea. Then "for reasons appearing to the court," the judges postponed her trial until April 17. The judges did not call the other two Harpe women before them, but postponed their trials until April 18.

Susan Harpe appeared in court again on April 17, and after hearing the same testimony as the prosecution presented at her hearing in January, a jury of twelve men found her guilty.

On the morning of April 18, a different jury heard exactly the same testimony against Betsey Harpe as the witnesses had presented against Susan Harpe the previous day. This jury took a different view and found Betsey Harpe not guilty.

That afternoon the judges took up the case of Sally Harpe and decided that they would "not further prosecute" her. They continued, "Therefore it is considered by the court that she is acquitted."

There was strangeness about everything to do with the Harpes. The trials of the Harpe women were no different. Even though the same witnesses presented the same evidence against all three, a jury found one "guilty," a second jury found one "not guilty," and the judges "acquitted" the third.

On April 19, Susan Harpe requested a new trial and the court granted it. Attorney General John Blair chose not to prosecute her again, however. He stated "certain of the reasons which moved him to enter into *nolle prosequi* [literally, "we shall no longer prosecute"] in this case." Blair reasoned that although Susan "has been found guilty of the charge in the indictment contained by a verdict of her peers" Betsey Harpe "was found not guilty" on the "same proof." Blair continued that because the court ordered a new trial, it was likely that a new jury would find her not guilty during the next term of court. He concluded that on "the advice of the prosecutor and of the Court, and also to save to the Commonwealth the expenses which attend her long detention and further prosecution, I have been induced to direct the Clerk to enter a nolle prosequi" against Susan Harpe.

Thus, there was no court-rendered punishment in the Langford case, even though the Harpe men each served 71 days in jail, Sally and Betsey Harpe 102 days each, and Susan Harpe 103 days. The cost to Logan County was considerable. Beyond feeding the prisoners and having four men hired to guard them, the county paid for the delivery of three children. Then, in the end, the murderers, and their accomplices, escaped justice.

It is understandable why the court at Danville refused to punish the Harpe women. The court, and the community at large, viewed the three as nothing more than victims of Micajah and Wiley Harpe. The three mothers had lived in distress and helplessness while in the clutches of the Harpe men. How horrible would a man have to be to force his pregnant wife to walk behind him on a frozen dirt path while he rode in relative comfort aboard a horse?

The people of Danville believed that the only positive outcome of the Langford murder was that the poor Harpe women had finally broken free of their barbarous husbands. Additionally, the maltreatment of their wives by the Harpes only intensified the community's desire to bring them to justice.

The Harpe women expressed no hard feelings toward the people of Kentucky. They told their former captors that their only desire was to return to Knoxville with their children and resume normal, peaceful lives. The townsfolk of Danville had pity for the women, and there were more than a little feelings of guilt generated from the knowledge that the women had spent the past three months in custody.

The people of Danville took up a collection for the women. The outpouring of sympathy and charity netted a considerable amount of clothing and a goodly sum of money for the former prisoners. Beyond that, a local man donated a horse for their use. It wasn't much of a horse, just an old mare long past its prime, fit for little more than use as a pack animal. Still, any horse was better than no horse, so reasoned the good folk of Danville.

The day the women left jail, each of them had a bundle of goods over her shoulder, an infant under her arm, and a little spending money. One of them led the old mare, loaded as it was with used clothing and bedding, out of town. The jailer, with the whole town watching, escorted the women to the edge of Danville and pointed out to them the road that led through Crab Orchard and on to Tennessee.

More than a few townsfolk prayed for the Harpe women before turning in for the evening. The trip back to Knoxville would be difficult and dangerous for strong men on good horses. Many wondered if perhaps they were actually sending the three exonerated Harpe women and their babies to their respective dooms. They shouldn't have worried. The Harpe women were resilient, and had no intention of returning to Tennessee.

9. On to Cave-In-Rock

NOT everyone viewed the Harpe women as forlorn victims simply trying to make their way back home. Some members of law enforcement believed that the women knew where Micajah and Wiley Harpe were, and that, if watched carefully, the women would soon lead authorities to the Harpe men.

The cynics were right. The Harpe women didn't return to Knoxville. After going fewer than thirty miles, the women turned west and followed the banks of the Green River in the opposite direction of Knoxville. Outlaws often hid out on the Green River and it gained the dubious distinction of "Rouge's Harbor."

A few days later, the women traded the old mare for a canoe and paddled down the stream. The spies following along behind the women lost track of them as they flowed down the winding river. The spies eventually gave up and returned home with no idea where the Harpe men were.

A few days after the Harpes escaped from jail, someone stumbled across the decomposed bodies of the travelers from Maryland. With all evidence pointing toward the Harpes, the citizens demanded the capture or extermination of the murderers before they could strike again.

The urgency of the case moved W. E. Strong, Justice of the Peace for Mercer County, to issue an order on March 28, instructing "all sheriffs and constables to take and recommit" the Harpes.

On April 22, the Commonwealth of Kentucky issued an order to the Lincoln County Sheriff Joseph Welsh to "take [Micajah and Wiley Harpe] who have lately broken the jail of this District and are now running at large." The order also commanded the sheriff "safely to keep [them] so that he have their bodies before the Judges of the District Court holden for the Danville District on the first day of their August Term, to answer for the felony and murder of a certain Thomas Langford whereof they stand indicted."

The locals did not think they could depend on the sheriff to capture the Harpes, or the jailer to keep them, or the court to convict them. From the middle of March 1799, citizens formed lynching parties and set out to search for the Harpes themselves.

A number of merchants, lawyers, and others did not approve of the illegal lynching parties roaming the countryside. These citizens sent a delegation to James Garrard, the Governor of Kentucky, and impressed upon him the urgent need to bring the Harpes to justice. The delegation's petition moved Garrard to action. Since the general belief was that the Harpes might have already reentered Tennessee, the governor issued a memo that "authorized Josh Ballenger to pursue them into the state of Tennessee and other states, and to apply to the executive authorities of such states to deliver them up."

Captain Joseph Ballenger had captured the Harpes once before, and he had confidence in his ability to take them again. Ballenger and his men did not wait to receive official sanction from the Governor to begin their pursuit of the outlaws. They moved down the trail with gusto to the headwaters of Rolling Fork, a branch of Salt River. There, they rode unknowingly directly into the Harpe camp. The outlaws were surprised, but not as startled as the posse. The Harpes grabbed their rifles and raised them to fire, which caused the frightened pursuers to scatter in disarray into the woods. By the time Ballenger had regrouped his force, the Harpes had gotten away.

Henry Skaggs is an important pioneer that history has all but forgotten. He was one of the "Long Hunters" that blazed trails through Tennessee and Kentucky with Colonel James Knox years earlier. It had been decades since he had forged through Kentucky the first time, and he had celebrated his 75th birthday just a few months before, but his fellows still considered Skaggs "a valiant man in battle and a great hunter."

When Ballenger had asked for volunteers, Skaggs had hastened to join the posse. Skaggs did not want to let the Harpes escape. He suggested the posse return with him to his nearby farm and then, with the aid of his fine hunting dogs, resume the chase. Most of the posse went with him and, using lanterns, they continued the search until long after nightfall.

Following the murderer's trail was difficult because it led the pursuers through a thicket of cane that was almost impenetrable. Finally, the men with Skaggs, all exhausted, and many discouraged, broke off the search and returned home.

In the meantime, Ballenger and a few men continued the search. Ballenger's contingent moved through an area that was free of heavy cane, but because the Harpes had not gone that way, their search was fruitless.

Skaggs didn't want the Harpes to get away because of a thick canebrake. The next day, he and Major James Blain went to the river a few miles north of the home of Colonel Daniel Trabue where several men were taking part in a "log rolling."

In those days, it was difficult to get logs out of forests so they could sell them. Lumbermen got around the problem by cutting down trees, removing their branches, and rolling the logs into rivers and floating them to market.

Skaggs and Blain tried to get the loggers to join them in another posse. The lumbermen refused to help find the Harpes. They stated that the cane was too thick and the chances of success too low to risk their lives going after the outlaws. The men wished Skaggs and Blain well and then they went back to their log rolling.

Skaggs was a persistent man. He decided to visit Colonel Daniel Trabue and enlist his help. Trabue, a veteran of the Revolutionary War, was also a prominent pioneer. He lived about three miles west of what is now Columbia,

Kentucky. Skaggs arrived at the Trabue home around April 10, 1799.

While Skaggs was going over his plans with Trabue, the Colonel was awaiting the return of his thirteen year old son, John. The lad went to a neighbor's house several hours earlier with his little dog to borrow flour and seed beans. The boy should have already been home, but if Trabue was overly worried, he didn't reveal it.

While Skaggs and Trabue talked, John's badly injured dog staggered into the front yard. Trabue and Skaggs went directly to the neighbor's home and received word that the boy had left there hours before with the seed beans and flour. The neighbor assured Trabue that the boy and the dog were uninjured when they departed for home.

The entire community searched for the boy for several days without finding any trace of the missing lad. Trabue feared that the Harpes had kidnapped his son John, but he had no proof of it. He was an intelligent man, and he knew that if the Harpes took the boy, and they had not already murdered him, they would certainly kill the child if someone did not find and capture them very soon.

George Spears and five other searchers found evidence of the Harpes about fifteen miles southwest of the Trabue farm, near the East Fork of the Barren River. The fugitives had slaughtered a calf and made moccasins from its skin. They tossed their old moccasins on the ground beside the remains of the calf and left the area. Spears and his party found footprints left by the Harpes, but there was no sign that John Trabue was with the criminals.

John Trabue had been missing for about two weeks when a person accidently found his mutilated body. A reconstruction of what had happened indicates that as the innocent boy walked down an old buffalo path toward home, the Harpes, who were walking across the path, spotted him. They attacked and killed the little fellow, dismembered him, and tossed his body into a sinkhole near the path. The Harpes took the flour for their trouble, but left the seed beans behind.

As might be expected, the loss of his son embittered Colonel Trabue. He blamed the loggers that refused to go with Skaggs and chase after the Harpes for the death of the child. Trabue wrote, "It is a pity they did not go, for then John Trabue might not have been killed." The Colonel added that after that, log rollers "reflected very much on themselves for their negligence, and said this ought to be a warning to others hereafter to always do their duty."

It wasn't fair for Colonel Trabue to criticize the woodsmen. They had no legal responsibility to stop their work and risk their lives chasing after the Harpes. Yet the truth is that the legal authorities on the American frontier did not have the means to maintain law and order in the wild country. They just didn't. The view prevailing at the time was that all honest citizens had a moral obligation to stamp out lawlessness when they could.

No one can say with certainly that had the log rollers gone with Skaggs, they would have captured the Harpes. No one can say that John Trabue would have avoided murder at the hands of the villains had the lumbermen gone after the Harpes. What is certain is that if private citizens had not volunteered to pursue the Harpes, their rampage may have gone on for years longer than it did. In fact, they might have avoided capture forever and escaped the frontier justice they so justly deserved. Had private citizens not intervened, the death toll may have risen to astronomical heights.

The knowledge that the Harpes were free and seemingly too sly for anyone to capture, unnerved the frontier folk in both Tennessee and Kentucky. The added knowledge that the mad dog killers would kill anyone in their path, even children, sent added chills down the spines of even the most hardened frontiersmen. All agreed that they could not remain sitting like serene ducks on a placid pond until the Harpes harvested them Yet a reasonable and safe course of action appeared elusive.

On April 22, a committee appealed again to Governor Garrard for help. The Governor responded by issuing the following proclamation:

BY THE GOVERNOR, A PROCLAMATION.

Whereas it has been represented to me that MICAJAH HARP, alias ROBERTS, and WILEY HARP alias ROBERTS, who were confined in the jail of the Danville district under a charge of murder, did on the 16th day of March last, break out of the said jail; – whereas the ordinary methods of pursuit have been found ineffectual for apprehending and restoring to confinement the said fugitives, I have judged it necessary to the safety and welfare of the community and to the maintenance of justice, to issue this my proclamation and do hereby offer and promise a reward of THREE HUNDRED DOLLARS to any person who shall apprehend and deliver into the custody of the jailer of the Danville district the said MICAJAH HARP alias ROBERTS and a like reward of THREE HUNDRED DOLLARS for apprehending and delivering as aforesaid the said WILEY HARP alias ROBERTS, to be paid out of the public treasury agreeably to law.

In testimony whereof I have hereunto set my hand and have caused the seal of the Commonwealth to be affixed.

Done at Frankfort on the 22nd day of April in the year of our Lord 1799, and of the Commonwealth the seventh.

(L. S.)

By the Governor JAMES GARRARD

Harry Toulmin, Secretary.

The Governor also issued a description of the criminals.

"MICAJAH HARP alias ROBERTS is about six feet high - of a robust make, and is about 30 or 32 years of age. He has an ill-looking, downcast countenance, and his hair is black and short, but comes very much down his forehead. He is built very straight and is full fleshed in the face. When he went away he had on a striped nankeen coat, dark blue woolen stockings – leggins of drab cloth and trousers of the same as the coat.

"WILEY HARP alias ROBERTS is very meagre in his face, has short black hair but not quite so curly as his brother's; he looks older, though really younger, and has likewise a downcast countenance. He had on a coat of the same stuff as his brother's, and had a drab surtout coat over the close-bodied one. His stockings were dark blue woolen ones, and his leggins of drab cloth."

While the Governor gave a rather detailed description of each of the Harpes, neither was altogether accurate. Firstly, The Harpes had to be older than the Governor surmised. Otherwise, Micajah Harpe would have been, at best, in his early teens when he fought for the British during the Revolution, and Wiley Harpe would have still been a preteen.

While it was possible for teenagers to serve in combat in the 18th Century, the two had already left home to pursue careers as slave overseers before the Revolution erupted, and no slaveholder would ever hire children for such an important duty as overseeing his collection of men in bondage.

Another description of Micajah Harpe stated, "His appearance was too striking not to rivet attention. In size he towered above the ordinary stature, his frame was bony and muscular, his breast broad, his limbs gigantic."

The thing that impressed people, especially potential enemies, about Micajah Harpe was his eyes. "The eye was fearless and steady, but it was also artful and audacious, glaring upon the beholder with an unpleasant fixedness and brilliancy, like that of a ravenous animal gloating upon its prey and concentrating all its malignity into one fearful glance." This ferocious gaze indicated pure villainy, and caused many a man to slink away in fear.

His face was remarkably large and he appeared devoid of human expression. His skin was not that of a normal man's. It was unnaturally red and appeared dried and lifeless.

Micajah Harpe was always heavily armed. He carried the rifle, powder horn, and pouch of the backwoodsman. He had a broad leather belt cinched closely about his waist. Inside his belt were two knives – one large, one small – and a tomahawk.

Micajah Harpe was not usually concerned about his dress. "His clothing was uncouth and shabby, His exterior weather beaten and dirty, indicating continual exposure to the elements, and pointing out this singular person as one who dwelt far from the habitations of men, and who mingled not in the courtesies of civilized life." He seldom wore a hat and his hair, black, curly, and usually long, remained matted and uncombed.

In short, Micajah Harpe appeared to be exactly what he was – "some desperate outlaw, an unnatural enemy of his species, destitute of the nobler sympathies of human nature, and prepared at all points for assault or defense."

Others said Micajah Harpe was "among the tallest class of men, say six feet two to six feet four inches" and with "sunken black eyes, a downcast, sour look; dark hair and high cheek bones."

The governor was also mistaken about Wiley Harpe. The younger Harpe "somewhat under common size, had" [red hair], blue eyes and a handsome look, but having the same suspicious exterior, his countenance equally fierce and sinister" as his brother.

Kentucky's newspapers gave Governor Garrard's proclamation the widest circulation possible, but paper and word of mouth did not move as quickly as the murderers did. Before the proclamation wound its way across the Bluegrass State, word came from Edmonton, in Metcalf County, that the Harpe brothers had murdered a man there named Dooley.

Then, the Harpes butchered a man named Stump on the Barren River about eight miles south of Bowling Green.

Stump was a poor, but friendly man. On the last day of his life, he was catching his supper at his favorite fishing spot. He noticed smoke coming from downstream a little ways. Stump assumed a new family of pioneers built the campfire preparatory to settling on an empty piece of land across the river. Happy to greet his new neighbors, Stump went to his cabin, put away his fishing pole, and took up his old fiddle and bow.

Stump wore a threadbare shirt and an old pair of pants. He owned no hat and only donned shoes in the wintertime. Unconcerned about his appearance, he tucked his fiddle and bow under his arm and, thinking his new neighbors might desire a good meal, he brought his stringer of fish along to share with them. Stump figured he would serenade the newcomers while they "cooked up" the fresh fish.

Old man Stump knew the river like the back of his hand, and he walked to a shallow crossing and waded across. Soon, he was in the camp. He likely never realized that he had walked into the viper's den of the most evil men in Kentucky. Sadly, he experienced the special kind of horror the Harpes wrought on even those offering them kindness.

Without a word, one of the Harpes struck Stump with such force that the old man went sprawling, and his fiddle and fish flew in different directions. As the little man, not understanding why he was under attack, attempted to rise, the Harpes descended upon him like wild animals upon prey, stabbing him multiple times. Stump's death was rather quick, but extremely painful.

After they had experienced the demented ecstasy that murders always brought them, the Harpes applied their signature disposal method to Stump. The cut open his chest cavity, filled it with heavy rocks, and then sank the innocent man's remains in the river.

At first, the authorities did not suspect the Harpes of murdering Mr. Stump. The local sheriff suspected that one of his neighbors had murdered him. He took a few of those living in the area into custody, but upon questioning, the evidence proved them innocent and he released them. Soon, the sheriff did have enough evidence to prove that the Harpes, still eluding arrest, had murdered the unfortunate Mr. Stump.

After murdering Stump, the bloody brothers moved along the Barren River and into the Green River country to a place near Henderson, Kentucky. There they reunited with their women. When they left Danville, the Harpe women headed to a predetermined hiding place to await Micajah and Wiley Harpe.

Battered Woman Syndrome, a subcategory of Post-Traumatic Stress Disorder, causes the abused to feel helpless and dependent on the abuser. The abused will also feel responsible for causing the abuse. Sometimes, women suffering from the condition will stay with, or return to, their abusers repeatedly, even though they know the abuse will continue, or even escalate.

It is impossible to know if the Harpe women suffered from Battered Woman Syndrome. But it is a plausible explanation as to why they returned to the terrible suffering they endured from the monstrous Harpe brothers, and clung to their companions in crime for as long as they did.

After reuniting, the five adults and three children moved quickly to the banks of the Ohio River. From there, they first went to

Diamond Island and after a few days, moved on to Cave-in-Rock. The number of men, women, and children that the Harpes murdered near Henderson is impossible to tell, but the facts prove that they committed several killings in the Green River country of the Ohio River Valley.

About twelve miles before they arrived at Cave-In-Rock, they were in Illinois near the mouth of the Saline River. They came upon three people sitting by a campfire. The Harpes drew their weapons, shot the unsuspecting campers several times, and left them dead on the scene.

Captain Ballenger had pursued the Harpes for weeks – or he thought he had pursued them. The truth was that Ballenger's posse got off the trail of the outlaws early on, and had been going in the wrong direction for almost the whole time they searched. When he realized his mistake, an embarrassed and despondent Ballenger released his men, abandoned the search, and returned home.

Captain Young from Mercer County, Kentucky, also organized a company of men to rid the area of criminals. Young's group, who promised "blood for blood," saw its mission as one to "exterminate the Harpes and all other outlaws, or at least drive them out of the country."

Captain Young's force swept through the mostly unmarked country of central and northern Kentucky, and succeeded in causing many criminals to flee before they arrived.

Having pushed most of the criminals out of Mercer County, Young's band continued on to Henderson County. There they reinforced their numbers with local volunteers and continued their drive to the Ohio River. From there, they landed on Diamond Island, causing the outlaws living there to flee across the river and into Illinois. Many of those displaced criminals sought shelter and security with the cutthroat pirates already using the place as a base for their criminal operation.

Captain Young's company was now 150 miles from home and they yearned to return. Declaring that his party had cleansed the area of the criminal element, Captain Young led his outlaw exterminators back to Mercer County, greeted by a welcome reserved only for heroes. However, lost in the adulation and fanfare was the fact that not only had Captain Young and his men not exterminated the Harpes, they never came close to capturing them. In fact, they never laid eyes on them.

Governor Garrard understood that the Harpes remained just as dangerous as ever, and he expected them to return to Kentucky if they believed that the Commonwealth had stopped pursuing them. In early June 1799, Garrard "deputed Alexander McFarland and brothers" to deal with "these inveterate enemies of human happiness" should they be located "in any adjacent state." Clearly, the Governor hoped that the continued vigilance of Kentuckians would keep the Harpes at bay.

As stated earlier, the Harpe women never intended to return to Knoxville. On the contrary, the women and their husbands had apparently planned a future rendezvous even before Micajah and Wiley Harpe managed their jailbreak. Either that or they somehow communicated with each other after the men took flight. Regardless, the women headed for where they expected them to arrive eventually.

As related earlier, the women canoed down the Green River some 200 miles until they arrived at its mouth. After stopping near Henderson for a short time, they paddled another 90 miles to Cave-in-Rock to meet the Harpe men. The trip of more than 300 miles through unknown territory from Danville to Cave-in-Rock was no small feat for the women, who were also caring for their infant children at the time. In fact, the treacherous journey might have been a subject of admiration had it been undertaken with pure intent.

At any rate, they started down Green River shortly after leaving Danville. They paddled their way along the river until they reached its mouth. After stopping in the neighborhood of Henderson, they continued down the Ohio about ninety miles to Cave-in-Rock. It was in this section of the Ohio Valley that they expected to meet the Harpe men, eventually.

After settling at Cave-in-Rock, the women separated. One went to a place south of Henderson, one went up the river to Diamond Island, and the third remained at Cave-in-Rock. The separation indicates that the women weren't certain exactly where the Harpe men would arrive, and they wanted to be sure that they didn't miss them.

Although there were no charges pending against any of them, the two Harpe women that departed Cave-in-Rock didn't reveal their real identities, but instead assumed aliases and claimed to be improvised widows. It is likely that the Harpe women returned to Cave-in-Rock before meeting their husbands because of Captain Young's raids at Henderson and Diamond Island.

Soon after the two women returned, the Harpe men arrived at Cave-in-Rock. The two men, three women, and three children probably lived there in May 1799.

Samuel Mason was the self-proclaimed "King of the River Pirates." His gang was the dominant element at Cave-in-Rock, and the Harpes went to work raiding flatboats floating the Ohio.

Young's crusade through Henderson County led to the extermination of some fifteen outlaws. While that was but a small fraction of the cutthroats in the area, Young and his posse caused a large number of other criminals and fugitives to abandon their hideouts and seek refuge in Cave-in-Rock. In a short time, so many outlaws resided in Cave-in-Rock that they were falling all over each other. The large number of bad men in one place made it unsafe for all of them. Because of that, most of the outlaws only stayed in Cave-in-Rock for a few days or weeks before moving down river, or making their way inland to safer and more secret environs. A relative few remained there "to pursue their nefarious avocation."

The Harpes left Cave-in-Rock too, but not of their own volition. The other criminals there drove them away. According to one author, "This aggregation of outlaws was doubtless a depraved conglomeration of evil doers, but in the Harpes they found two human brutes beyond even their toleration."

The Harpes had only been at Cave-in-Rock a matter of days when they committed an act that shocked and repulsed even their criminal comrades. A flatboat floated down the Ohio River and those aboard, not knowing they were near a den of vipers, decided to stop for a bit and make repairs to the vessel. They directed their conveyance to the shore about a quarter of a mile above Cave-in-Rock at the bottom of a bluff, later called Cedar Point. There they tethered the damaged flatboat and commenced work on it.

Two of the travelers were young sweethearts, and as one might expect, they sneaked away from the repair party for some private time. The young lovers meandered to the top of Cedar Point and found a large, smooth rock on which to sit and view the lovely river as it rushed past. While the two sat with their backs to the thick woods, the Harpe brothers came up from behind quietly and committed what they considered a prank.

Without warning, the brothers grabbed the boy and girl and threw them over the ledge. The lovers fell some forty feet to the sandy beach below. Amazingly, neither of the victims suffered serious injury.

The Harpes rushed back to Cave-in-Rock to brag about their practical joke, but to their surprise, the other pirates found nothing funny about the unnecessary and pointless attack perpetrated by the demented brothers. The other outlaws understood that there was no profit in wanton acts of violence, and such acts would accomplish nothing but to bring attention to the band of cutthroats.

After the bad reaction they received, the Harpes should have been more cautious about unnecessary maliciousness. They were not. Shortly after throwing the sweethearts off the bluff, the Harpes engaged in another, even more disgusting, display of senseless brutality.

Two families were moving down the Ohio River in a flatboat. They intended to settle at a place called Smithland. These pioneers brought tools and provisions to sustain them until they had established themselves in their new homes.

When the families and their loaded flatboat floated near Cave-in-Rock, the river pirates fell upon them. The pioneers fought back, but they were no match for the criminals. The pirates killed most of those on the flatboat, but spared two or three and brought them ashore as captives.

The Harpe brothers saw the helpless kidnapped victims as a potential source of fun. One of the Harpes forced a captive to strip down naked while the other Harpe blindfolded a horse. Then, the two tied the naked man on top of the frightened animal and led it to the top of the cliff above the cave. Next, the Harpes began "hooting and hollering." The sound of the wild shouts startled the blindfolded horse, it bolted forward, and over the cliff, taking the man tied to its back over the ledge too. The poor horse and man fell more than 100 feet to the rocky shore below. The resulting carnage was beyond description.

The Harpes enjoyed their game and took pride in their handiwork. The other pirates, although murderers themselves, felt repulsed by this crime. Not one of the other criminals had ever witnessed such a horrible sight before, and none of them wanted to see such a sight again.

Some of the pirates suggested killing the Harpes in retribution for this horrible murder, but apparently the Harpe women interceded and convinced Samuel Mason not to leave them widowed mothers with infant children. Instead of killing Micajah and Wiley Harpe, Samuel Mason demanded they leave at once. Outnumbered and with no other recourse, the Harpes departed.

It was true that Captain Young had driven the Harpes out of Kentucky and into Illinois. Now, in May 1799, the good citizens of the Commonwealth hoped – prayed – they had seen the last of the Harpes. The Kentuckians expected the Harpes to continue north, or to find their way to the Mississippi River and flow with it to Louisiana.

10. The Spree Continues

THE general opinion of east Tennesseans was that Harpes had abandoned the area permanently. They thought that not even fugitives as foolhardy and arrogant as the Harpes would return to the area after such a short absence. They were wrong. The Harpes did not flee north or west from Cave-In-Rock, but east back into Tennessee.

In the middle of July 1799, word circulated that a farmer named Bradbury suffered a vicious death at the hands of murderers. The killing took place in Roane County on Bradbury's Ridge. Bradbury's Ridge was about 25 miles west of Knoxville. At first, no one suspected the Harpes of killing Bradbury.

On July 22, mere days after the Bradbury murder, they struck again. This victim was the young son of Chesley Coffey, on Black Oak Ridge, about eight miles northwest of Knoxville.

There are two versions of how the Harpes took Coffey's life. The first story is that the boy was on foot late one afternoon rounding up cattle that had strayed into the woods when the Harpes jumped out from the shadows, surprising and killing the lad. Then they took his rifle and his shoes, and left the murdered boy under a tree.

The second version is that "Young Coffey was riding along the road one evening to get a fiddle. These terrible men smeared a tree with his brains, making out that his horse had run against the tree."

Regardless of their method, the horrible Harpes were back, and their bloodlust remained unquenchable.

Two days after ambushing Coffey, the Harpes struck again, this time killing William Ballard, who lived just a few miles from Knoxville. They left their calling card with Ballard when "They cut him open and, putting stones in his body, sank it in the river." Locals surmised that Ballard was not really the target, and that the Harpes mistook him for Hugh Dunlap. Dunlap had gained notoriety in his efforts to arrest the brothers during the previous year.

The Harpes continued their bloody migration northward. The dastards crossed the Emery River near Harriman Junction, where the women made camp in a secluded area deep in the woods. While the women rested a few days in the hideout, the men continued alone into Morgan County. They took their next victim on July 29, at a place called Brassel's Knob.

On this hot summer day, brothers James and Robert Brassel were travelling slowly along, not far from their home. James was on foot and carrying his rifle. Robert – unarmed and on horseback – rode along beside his brother.

Micajah and Wiley Harpe, both astride fine stallions, approached the Brassel brothers from the opposite direction. That is, the Harpes were coming from Knoxville. At first, the murderous duo pretended to be in a hurry, but then they slowed their horses to a stop and asked the men, "What's the news?"

The Brassel brothers had plenty of news to relate to the strangers. They told the men in gory detail about the slayings of William Ballard and the Coffey boy. The Harpes nodded grimly and said that not only were they aware of the murders, but they were part of a posse hot on the trail of the villains. They continued that they had been scouting ahead of the rest of the pack.

The Harpes said they were going to wait for the remainder of the posse to catch up. Then, they asked the Brassel brothers if they would join them when the other pursuers arrived.

The Brassels did not question why the two men, who seemed to be in such a hurry just minutes before, were now content to wait for reinforcements. The naïve brothers, excited by the prospect of the chase, agreed to join the search.

Within seconds of the Brassels agreeing to join the fake posse, Micajah Harpe grabbed James Brassel's rifle, slamming it to the ground. He then accused the innocent men of being the much hated Harpes. Micajah Harpe then began tying James Brassel's hands and feet together. The bewildered man proclaimed his innocence, but he did not put up very much resistance.

Robert Brassel finally realized the men accosting them were the Harpes. He leapt from his horse and went after his brother's gun. Finding his path to the weapon blocked, Robert ran into the woods to save himself, leaving his horse behind. Wiley Harpe chased after Robert and shot at the horrified man, but missed. Robert Brassel was younger and better conditioned than Wiley Harpe was, and he outmaneuvered the bloodthirsty murderer in the thick foliage.

Robert ran like a lunatic through the woods, thinking that the Harpes would grab him any second. After a bruising sprint of about ten miles, he came upon a man named Dale. Dale was on his way to Knoxville with his wife and two or three men. Brassel begged them to return with him to the place where he left his brother, and they reluctantly agreed to do so. They only had one gun between them, and they knew they could not withstand the firepower the outlaws possessed. Nor did they love spilling blood the way the psychotic Harpes did. Yet they went along with Robert.

When Robert and the others were a short distance from where he had left his brother James, they found the man dead. The sight of seeing James on the ground, his body "much beaten and his throat cut," unnerved those that saw it. Besides mutilating James Brassel, the Harpes shattered his rifle to pieces, making it useless to anyone who should find it.

Robert Brassel and the others noticed that the tracks left by the Harpes were heading back toward Knoxville.

The pursuers followed the tracks, but Dale and his companions were in no hurry to catch up to the villains. Then a few miles down the trail, the pursuers were shocked to see the Harpes riding back towards them.

The Harpes had been alone when they attacked the Brassel brothers. Now they had their women and children with them. Unlike as was usual, the women were on horseback. Beyond that, they had a heavy load of clothing and other provisions. Apparently, the Harpes had gone to their hideout where their women waited, and then started out on what they figured to be a long trip. The Harpes were heavily armed and appeared ready for combat.

As the murderers approached, Dale's men became ever more unnerved. One of the pursuers suggested that if the Harpes did not start a gunfight with them, they should make no effort to arrest the outlaws. Fearing they would suffer the same fate as James Brassel, the other members of Dale's party agreed not to fight unless necessary. Robert Brassel disagreed with the decision, but he had no weapon and could not do anything on his own.

As the Harpes passed their pretended pursuers on the road, they certainly recognized Robert Brassel but made no move towards him. As to the others, the Harpes "looked very awful at them" and rode past without a word.

The cowardly party continued towards Knoxville, but they didn't speak until they were sure that they were out of earshot of the Harpes. They were afraid that if they made any utterance, the Harpes would view it as a threat, turn back, and attack them.

When Dale's men finally broke their silence, Robert Brassel expressed his anger and disappointment at the men. He said he had depended upon them to help him take vengeance against his brother's murderers, but they were too timid to do anything.

Cowardly or not, Dale's men were wise not to challenge the Harpes. With only one rifle between them, there was no way they could have outbattled the murderers. The outlaws were experienced warriors, and they loved to spill blood. If Dale's men had engaged in a skirmish, the Harpes would have added several other names to their bloody list of victims.

By this time, eastern Tennessee was in an uproar. The knowledge that the Harpes had again infested their countryside put the entire population on edge. The Harpes might strike anywhere at any time, and the people felt they had no choice except to be prepared to fight back, if necessary. Men, women, and children armed themselves with guns, hunting knives, daggers, frying pans – anything they could use as weapons.

Having avoided trouble immediately after killing James Brassel, the Harpes, with their women and plunder, pointed their horses towards the west, intent on slipping back into Kentucky. Yet they tarried long enough to murder in the Volunteer State again. In Pickett County, barely on the Tennessee side of the state line, they swooped down and killed John Tully, a Kentucky resident.

Robert Brassel did not accept the fact that the Harpes had gotten away. Soon after the encounter with them, he resumed his pursuit of the bloody brothers. William Wood and others joined Brassel in his mission to either bring the Harpes to justice, or slay the monstrous dragons. Brassel would have preferred to see them dead.

Brassel and his men met Nathaniel Stockton and a group of other men near the Tully farm. Stockton explained that he and the others were searching for John Tully. Tully had been missing for some time, and Stockton feared that he was lost in the woods. It was easy to lose one's way in the forest, and once lost, it was difficult to find one's bearings again. Even the great Daniel Boone is quoted as saying, "I can't say as ever I was lost, but I was bewildered once for three days." Understanding that the man might be in great danger, Brassel and his posse agreed to help look for Tully.

After a short search "near the road they found Mr. Tully, killed, and hidden under a log." They buried Tully, and certain that the Harpes were the culprits, some of Stockton's men joined Brassel's troop and took up the search for the serial killers.

This murder was not committed simply for the devilish joy the Harpes took from slaughtering their fellowmen. The Harpes had a reason for killing John Tully. Although the precise reason they targeted him is uncertain, there is no doubt that they sought Tully out to murder him.

John Tully was a man of some stature in his community. He settled 200 acres of good land in Kentucky, and married a good woman named Christiana, who bore him eight children. Yet there was another side to this otherwise law-abiding citizen. He had known the Harpes for sometime. Less than a year before they killed him, he had delivered messages to the murderous brothers from their wives as the men made their way to Cave-in-Rock.

There is no evidence as to why Tully helped the pair of butchers. It may have been that his motives were pure. Regardless of his reasons for becoming acquainted with the Harpes, it cost him his life.

Immediately after finding John Tully, William Wood and Nathaniel Stockton began a forty-mile trek afoot to Colonel Daniel Trabue's farm. Wood and Stockton thought that since Trabue had searched for the Harpes after they murdered his son, the murderers might be going to the Colonel's home or his general store to kill him. They reasoned that if this was true, they might capture the unsuspecting outlaws at the Trabue place.

Upon their arrival, Wood and Stockton related the most recent outrages committed by the butchering Harpe brothers to Colonel Trabue. Trabue, who was a Justice of the Peace for Green County, felt that the next best step was to forward news of the recent murders to the Kentucky Governor.

Trabue prepared a written report based on the sworn statements he received from Wood and Stockton, giving a description the four latest murders. The statement began, "About the middle of July there was a man killed by the name of Hardin, about three miles below Knoxville: he was ripped open and stones put in his belly, and he was thrown into Holston River." There is no record of the Harpes killing a man named Hardin at that time. Evidently, Trabue either referred to the murder of William Ballard, or the Hardin murder never made the official records.

Next, the statement recounted the killing of Chesley Coffey's son, James Brassel, and John Tully.

In his affidavit, Colonel Trabue provided a description of the Harpes that differed somewhat from other descriptions. Trabue stated that "The big man is pale, dark, swarthy, bushy hair, had a reddish gun stock – little man had a blackish gunstock, with a silver star with four straight points – they had short sailor's coats, very dirty, and grey greatcoats."

Colonel Trabue prepared two handwritten copies of the statement during the evening. At daybreak the next morning, he sent a rider to Frankfort, about 100 miles to the north, to deliver it to Governor Garrard. Trabue hoped the Governor would give his statement the widest circulation possible.

Colonel Trabue directed another man, John Ellis, to travel the 200 or so miles to Henderson (aka "Red Banks") and deliver the statement to General Samuel Hopkins.

Trabue ordered the riders to go as quickly as possible and spread the news among as many people as they could that the Harpes were back in Kentucky. According to Trabue, "Ellis had a good horse and went sixty or seventy miles a day." That may have been an overstatement, but Ellis did make good time on the road toward Henderson.

Apparently, the Harpes intended to return to Cave-in-Rock, because they were traveling towards Henderson and when they got wind of what Ellis was doing, they attempted to overtake and murder him. However, they couldn't catch up to him.

The two messengers Colonel Trabue sent out on their arduous journeys had many dangers ahead of them other than the Harpes. The road was bad, and if a horse took a misstep and threw its rider, the poor man, even if he survived the fall, might expire on the ground before anyone found him. Besides that, a stampeding buffalo herd, or an overprotective mother bear, might mean the end of a rider. Perhaps the greatest danger was getting lost on the path that passed for a road. It was rather common for lost persons to wander in the forest for days, and to die from exposure without regaining their bearings.

Trabue's messengers were good men. They spread the news with the gusto of a March wind, and soon almost the whole of Kentucky became aware of the renewed Harpe menace. The alarming news filtered back into Tennessee as well.

The word that the barbarous Harpes were cutting a new path of murder and destruction through Kentucky threw the Commonwealth into a state approaching hysteria. The citizens knew the Harpes were in Kentucky, but not where. Thus, no one felt safe. Beyond that, perhaps every community in Kentucky had witnesses swear they saw the murderers nearby. Most believed the reports to be nothing more than rumors, but they did not have the luxury of discounting the reports either. It was a frightful time for the pioneers in Kentucky.

The fear of the Harpes spilled out of Kentucky and Tennessee to other states as well. Reports of the nefarious exploits gained circulation as far north as Cincinnati, Ohio, and as far east as Charleston, South Carolina.

Newspapers flamed the fears of the populace by reporting rumors as fact and by engaging in hyperbolic statements. It is also true that newspapers sometimes tried to encourage the beleaguered Kentuckians. On August 15, 1799, *The Frankfort Palladium* stated about the Harpes, "We are happy to hear they are closely pursued and sincerely hope they will ere long meet the punishment which the atrocity of their crimes demands."

Despite all the precautions Kentuckians took to protect themselves from the Harpes, the vicious monsters still managed to find victims. The day after Colonel Trabue's riders sped off to Frankfort and Henderson, the Harpes were making their way up Marrowbone Creek about twenty-five miles south of the Colonel's home. The Harpes stopped at a small cabin belonging to John Graves. Graves and his thirteen-year-old son were working their small farm. They planned for the rest of their family to join them soon.

The Graves farm was miles away from any other homestead. When the Harpes arrived at the cabin after dark, they awakened the man and boy, and asked to spend the night. John Graves allowed it. Sensing no danger, Graves and his son went quickly back to sleep and slumbered soundly, not knowing they would be dead in a matter of hours.

The most authoritative account of the next morning follows:

"Early in the morning, probably before the [the man and boy] awoke, they, with Graves' own axe, split the heads of both open and threw the bodies of both in to the brush fence that surrounded the house. There they lay until someone, seeing so many buzzards around, made an investigation and discovered what had taken place."

From the Graves cabin, the Harpes, with their women and children, moved a little over twenty miles north into Russell County. There they stayed for a short period with a man referred to mythically as "Old Man Roberts."

Legends persist that this person was the father of the two women Micajah Harpe claimed as his wives. Of course, this is impossible. "Old Man Roberts" could not have been the father of either of the women. We know that at least one of the women was the daughter of Captain James Wood, and we know that the Harpes kidnapped both women in North Carolina. It is inconceivable that even if "Old Man Roberts" had moved to Kentucky from North Carolina, that he would have welcomed the kidnappers of his daughter into his home years later. After staying a few days with "Old Man Roberts," the Harpes fled southwest of Green River toward Mammoth Cave and Russellville.

As the Harpes travelled in the direction of Logan County, they committed others murders. First, they killed a slave. The account of the murder went, "They met with a negro boy going to mill, dashed the boy's brains out against a tree, but left the horse and bag of grain untouched."

They next killed a little girl. The record states, "One of their victims was a little girl found at some distance from her home, whose tender age and helplessness would have been protection against any but incarnate fiends." According to those that viewed the child, before the Harpes left the scene they cut the little girl's body into one-inch strips.

Two members of the Cherokee tribe accompanied the Harpes into Logan County, Kentucky. Exactly when the Cherokees joined up with the Harpes, or why the Harpes accepted them, is uncertain. They may have been friends the Harpes made when they lived among the Natives, but it is uncertain. Regardless, they arrived in Logan County after nightfall and came across a camp about eight miles from what is now Adairville, Kentucky.

The inhabitants of the camp were two brothers named Trisword, their wives, and others.

The Harpes and their Cherokee confederates lurked in the darkness until just before dawn, when they attacked the campers who all slept in one large tent. The merciless slaughter continued for several minutes, and only one man escaped the melee alive.

The man who avoided the massacre ran for help. When he returned with a rescue party, they found, sprawled on the blood-soaked campground, the badly mutilated bodies of the seven unfortunate travelers that could not escape the horror that the Harpes and their cohorts brought upon them.

Several members of the rescue party took on the unenviable task of digging shallow graves and burying the victims. Ruing still another tragedy visited upon the world by the Harpes, other members of the party searched for tracks left by the villains. They found evidence that the Harpes were headed southward in the direction of Tennessee.

Upon learning of the massacre, Logan County Sheriff William Stewart hastily organized a posse of about a dozen men and dashed toward the state line. Sadly, they were going in the wrong direction.

The Harpes were as cunning as they were ruthless, and they left false tracks to deceive their pursuers. The trick worked, and as the posse flew toward the Tennessee border, the Harpes ambled northwardly.

With the luxury of moving with ease, the Harpes stopped to water their horses about three miles northeast of Russellville, near the Mud River, on the Russellville and Morgantown Road. It was now August 1799.

The large spring where their horses drank was the central point of many outside meetings. Mere weeks before, the Presbyterian Reverends John and William McGee and James McGready conducted their "Great Revival" on that very spot. This was the first of the Great Revivals that set the West ablaze with renewed religious fervor. One participant described thusly: "Fires were built, cooking begun, and by dark candles lighted and fixed on a hundred trees around and interspersing the ground surrounded by tents, showing forth the first, and as I believe still, one of the most beautiful camp meetings the world has ever seen."

The Harpes likely realized the grounds around the spring had been the locale of a recent religious event. If they did, it did not affect them; they didn't consider the place hallowed ground. In fact, it became the scene of one of their most hideous and gruesome crimes.

The Harpes held no affection for anyone, not even their own children. In fact, they often expressed a desire to rid themselves of the burdens their babies caused them. It infuriated them when the children cried. The outlaws feared that the "bawling young'uns" would someday attract a posse to them and cause their capture. Many times, the Harpe men threatened to slaughter the children before the babies attracted sharp-eared pursuers to their location.

The Harpe women knew their men didn't engage in idle threats, and that their children were always in mortal danger. Often, just after nightfall, the women carried the babies far enough from camp to keep the Harpe men from hearing the children cry. Of course, it is impossible to keep babies from crying, and it was impossible for the Harpe women to protect the innocent children forever. It was simply a matter of time before a frightful tragedy occurred.

In an irony that was likely lost on Micajah Harpe, he committed his most senseless – and most deplorable – crime on the very grounds where so many had just recently given themselves to the Lord.

The accepted story of the deed goes this way: Micajah Harpe's infant daughter was very hungry and she started crying. The child's incessant wailing angered him, and he decided to quiet the little girl. "Big Harpe snatched it – Susan's infant, about nine months old – from its mother's arms, slung it by the heels against a large tree by the path side, and literally bursting its head into a dozen pieces, threw it from him as far as his great strength enabled him, into the woods."

Micajah Harpe, it seems, took no notice of the little girl's blood dripping from the large maple tree.

Apparently, Susan Harpe was too terrified of her husband to stand up to him. There is no evidence that she made any complaint when he murdered their daughter and tossed the child's body into the woods.

11. The End of Micajah Harpe

THE Harpes knew that a growing number of men were after them, intending to chase them across Kentucky. Despite the fact they knew their pursuers were gaining on them, the Harpes continued to leave a trail of death and destruction that a blind man could follow. It seemed that increasing their body count was more important to them than getting away.

Those chasing the Harpes couldn't quite catch them, but the general belief was that the outlaws had left the Russellville area and were on their way to West Tennessee, perhaps even to the Mississippi Territory. This being the case, there was a collective sigh of relief and a letting down of their guards in the area. Within days, most residents stopped worrying about the bloody brothers. Again, the Harpes had managed to fool their adversaries and potential victims.

The Harpes, with their women and two remaining babies, did not migrate to western Tennessee at all. Instead, they eased back into Henderson County, Kentucky, and rented a cabin on a small farm adjoining Canoe Creek. Their new residence was about eight miles south of Henderson.

There were large salt licks in the area, including Robertson's Lick and Highland Lick near the mouth of Highland Creek. Knob Lick (a few miles east of the others) was near what is now Sebree, Kentucky, in Webster County. Salt was an essential commodity in pioneer times, and because of the abundance of natural salt wells and "salt works" in the area, it became a prime location for migrants from the east.

Because of the constant flow of people getting salt along Highland Lick Road and its adjacent pathways, then returning home, strangers in the area attracted virtually no attention. Beyond that, Captain Young's blood-for-blood crusade had cleared out the criminal element in Henderson County, and no highwayman would have the audacity to return, or so the locals thought.

No one paid much regard when the strangers moved into Canoe Creek. The owner of the farm and cabin had rented them before, but no one had remained there more than a season or two. Of course, no one suspected that the new residents, dirty and wearing rags, were the repulsive Harpes. Everyone had heard of the Harpes, and there was a good description of them floating about. Yet the description could have matched many of the newcomers drifting into Henderson County. The area attracted many more down-on-their-luck, poorly dressed, unwashed pioneers than it did debutants and well-to-do lawyers.

Another reason no one considered the possibility that the new settlers were the Harpes was because no one conceived that the murderers could still be in the country. Their neighbors saw these newcomers as what they appeared to be – pioneers trying to wrestle a meager existence from the ground by the sweat of their brows.

John Slover was a local legend in Henderson County. He had gained a degree of fame as an "Indian fighter" in eastern Kentucky. His daring escape from Native Americans holding him captive grew into a romantic story of mythical proportions. While Slover never gained the national status of Daniel Boone or some of the other frontier heroes, he was, in his circle, a big man.

Slover lived about a mile from the cabin that the Harpes leased, but he had only seen them a couple of times, and on those occasions, he was too far away from them to make out their features. Thus even if he had been on the lookout for the Harpes, he would not have recognized these strangers as the villains.

Slover had also gained renown as a hunter. One day near Robertson's Lick, he bagged a bear not far from the path that led back to his house. He ended his successful hunt, went back to the path, and began to ride home slowly. As he rode along, he heard the snap of a rifle hammer. Luckily for him, the weapon did not fire.

Realizing he was in danger, Slover wheeled around and saw the heavily armed Micajah and Wiley Harpe, "wilder looking than Indians in battle," staring at him. The men were more ferocious than any wild beast Slover had ever encountered, and he did not waste any time analyzing the situation. He spurred his horse and rode away from the murderous men as quickly as his horse would carry him. The Harpes chose not to give chase, and Slover escaped unharmed.

Slover told some of the men in the area about the failed murder attempt. He stated his opinion that his assailants were the infamous Harpe brothers. Slover had a reputation for honesty, and his friends believed the story about his narrow escape. They didn't believe the would-be murderers were the Harpes, however. He could not convince them that even men as bold and bloodthirsty as the Harpes would hazard a return to this place so recently washed clean of hoodlums. Slover didn't change his mind either. He was certain he had been face to face with the most vicious men in the United States.

Had his friends listened to Slover, a man named Trowbridge may have survived. Mere days after Slover's near-fatal run-in with the Harpes, Trowbridge departed Robertson's Lick with a load of salt. His destination was a farm that hugged the Ohio River near the mouth of Highland Creek. No one ever saw Trowbridge alive again.

When Trowbridge didn't return, fears rose in the community, but no one found him or his body. In fact, his mysterious disappearance may have remained an eternal mystery had not one of the Harpe women admitted what had happened to the poor salt teamster. Months after the killing, she related that the Harpes came upon Trowbridge about eight miles from the mouth of Highland Creek and slaughtered him. Then, as they so often did to their victims, they ripped open his chest cavity, filled it with stones, and sunk the corpse into the stream. In this case, the rocks remained in place and he stayed on the bottom of the tributary.

General Samuel Hopkins intended to keep another criminal hoard from descending upon the country again. When word came to him about the failed attack on Slover, Hopkins acted. He did not believe the scourge of Kentucky had returned, but he didn't want to take any chances either. He tasked a number of men to watch the cabin on Canoe Creek and report what they saw there.

It is interesting that no matter where they were, the Harpes always had allies willing to help them. As already noted on many occasions, the Harpes had confederates tip them off just before pursuers caught up to them. In this instance too, they had allies in the community. Somehow, the Harpes learned spies were watching them.

The Harpes changed their attire and their appearance to the degree that they looked very different than they did when Slover saw them. Keeping low and out of sight, Slover crawled up to where the spies were keeping vigil and got another look at the Harpes, but their appearance was so different that he could not be sure they were the same men that tried to ambush him.

The clever Harpes knew it was not safe to leave their rented abode as long as they were under surveillance. They maintained the pretense of being hardworking farmers and bided their time.

Other than the absence of the women, those watching the Harpes saw nothing much out of the ordinary at the farm. Later, those pursuing the Harpes learned that before the spies took up their positions, the murderers had ordered the women to one of their many hideouts to await them.

After about a week of sleeping on the ground and enduring both sweltering days and heavy rain showers, the spies gave up their surveillance and returned to their homes, hot meals, and soft beds. The spies never realized the Harpes knew they were there, or that the outlaws thoroughly enjoyed the sport of deceiving them.

On August 21, the day after the spies departed, the Harpe men abandoned their cabin and began the ride to the hiding place where the women and their children waited. The Harpes rode southwardly about fifteen miles until they came to the home of James Tompkins on Deer Creek. The Tompkins farm was near a place then called Steuben's Lick.

There was a story that Revolutionary War hero, General Friedrich Wilhelm von Steuben, suffered a wound there in the early 1780s in a battle with Native Americans. There is no evidence that the tradition of the battle is true, but the locals took pride in the legend.

The Harpes, as related earlier, had traded their old, flea-ridden garments for clothing that was more becoming in order to fool the spies.

When they met Tompkins, they were dressed well enough to fit into "good company." Adding to the pretense that they were gentlemen, they rode strong, healthy horses, and when they represented themselves to Tompkins as Methodist ministers, he believed them. The fact that the faux preachers were heavily armed did not concern Tompkins. The frontier was a dangerous place, and even men of God usually carried weapons when they roamed the wilderness.

The Harpes seemed friendly and engaging, and wanting to be a good Christian, Tompkins felt it his duty to invite the preachers to share his evening meal and they accepted. Tompkins asked the preachers to say grace over supper, and Micajah Harpe gave a long blessing that their host found most acceptable.

During their repast, the Harpes made what appeared to be idle conversation with their host. One of them asked him about the amount of venison he had. Tompkins replied that he had none. He said he hadn't hunted for several days because he had no powder for his gun.

Under usual circumstances, the Harpes would have murdered the defenseless man, but this day they did something out of character. Micajah Harpe decided to repay the generous Tompkins with a favor. With his big right hand, Harpe pulled a teacup towards him, took his powder horn, pulled out the wooden stopper, and filled the cup to the brim with dry black powder. Ironically, Micajah Harpe paid dearly for this singular act of kindness.

The Harpes never made an aggressive move toward Tompkins. When he invited them to stay for the evening, they declined politely. The Harpes told their accommodating host that they could not tarry overnight, as they had an appointment several miles to the south which they could not neglect. Tompkins assumed the appointment dealt with their ministerial duties, and he wished them well on their journey. The Harpes thanked Tompkins for his courtesy, mounted their horses, and took the southward trail.

The Harpes did have an appointment, but it had nothing to do with religion – it was all about murder.

They spared Tompkins because they were in a hurry to get to another man they had already targeted for death. After leaving Tompkins, the Harpes rode by the soft, glowing moonlight for a short distance, then turned to the northwest and made for the farm owned by Squire Silas McBee. McBee lived about one-half mile from Tompkins.

Unlike most pioneers in the frontier, thirty-four year old Silas McBee was highly educated and politically well-connected. He was also a man of action. He took part in the Revolutionary War battle of Kings Mountain when he was only fifteen. Later, he fought in other Revolutionary War battles and in various Indian wars. He was also a successful hunter and farmer, and he acquired substantial wealth.

It is interesting and ironic that McBee and the Harpe brothers fought on different sides of the Battle of Kings Mountain. Of course, McBee and the Harpes never saw one another, and the animosity between them had nothing to do with the battle. It developed years later.

Sometime in the early 19th Century, McBee moved to Alabama and served as a member in that state's first legislature. He then moved to Mississippi and lived the remainder of his life there.

McBee's daughter, Sarah, married Tilghman Mayfield Tucker, and when he won election as Governor, she served as First Lady of Alabama. Another of McBee's daughters married Thomas Hill Williams and resided with him in our nation's capital during the time he represented Alabama in the United States Senate.

In 1799, McBee was a Justice of the Peace. He had been a leader of the effort to rid the community of outlaws. The Harpes intended to butcher McBee in retribution for his attempts to kill, capture, or drive them away. They figured it would be easy enough to rip McBee to pieces. They believed that McBee's mutilated body would serve as a warning to anyone that might consider pursuing them.

It was still early evening when they arrived at McBee's property, but the occupants were already in bed. The Harpes crept close to the house, but a surprise awaited them. McBee had six or so ill-tempered hound dogs he used to hunt bear and deer. When the hounds became aware of the Harpes, they attacked. The dogs were on the Harpes before the men could raise their rifles, and the murderers were forced to defend themselves with their bare hands.

The noise of the fight between the murderers and the pack of dogs shook McBee from his slumber. He rose, went to his door, and peered into his moonlit yard. Ordinarily, he would have called off the ferocious beasts, but his intuition told him that the men under attack were there for evil purposes, and he allowed the dogs to continue to protect his home. In a short time, the hounds proved too much for them, and the Harpes quit the fight. They scrambled to their horses and the dogs ripped at the Harpes until the men rode away to safety.

The Harpes were lucky that the sharp-toothed hounds only inflicted minor wounds upon them. After escaping the dogs, the Harpes needed a place to spend the night. They could have returned to the Tompkins home, but they knew of a safer place to spend the evening. They rode about four miles to the northwest, to the cabin of Moses Stegall. The Stegall homestead sat about five miles east of what is now Dixon, Kentucky.

The Harpes knew exactly where Stegall lived. On August 16, the three Harpe women, appearing to be travelling alone, stopped at John Leiper's house and asked for directions to Moses Stegall's farm. Isom Sellers was there, and Susan Harpe asked him for the dollar he owed her. He advised her to get the money from Stegall when she saw him. Stegall later confirmed that he did pay Susan the dollar that Sellers owed her.

It is interesting how many area folk knew and did business with the outlaws. No information exists as to how Isom Sellers came to owe Susan Harpe money, or why Stegall felt obligated to make good the debt. However, it confirms that Sellers had done business with the outlaws (or their wives), and lends credence to the rumors that Stegall served as a spy or messenger for the Harpes. It also proves that Stegall had contact with the Harpes a few days before they visited his home on August 21.

On the evening of August 21, Moses Stegall was not at home, but his wife Mary and their son James were. The child was only four-months-old.

The Stegall home had another visitor that evening. A surveyor named Major William Love came to the house a few hours earlier to see Moses Stegall on business. Mary Stegall told Love that she expected her husband to return before morning, and she asked him to remain until her absent husband made his way back there. Love said he was tired from the long excursion of the day, and she said he could rest in the loft of the house. He climbed the ladder that was on the outside of the house, went into the loft, and collapsed in the only bed there.

Love did not rest long before he heard the Harpes ride up outside. When Mrs. Stegall invited them in, Love climbed down, reentered the house, and greeted the visitors as well.

The Stegalls had previously lived in Knox County, Tennessee, and they knew the Harpes well. The outlaws had informed Mrs. Stegall previously to avoid addressing them by their real names if another person was present. Mrs. Stegall introduced the Harpes to Major Love by using one of their many aliases, and the surveyor never knew he was in the presence of notorious desperados.

As was their way, the Harpes feigned innocence. The outlaws asked Love about the Harpes, who said that there were stories burning across the countryside that the cutthroats were close by. However, Love said he doubted that the Harpes were prowling around the area, and that he wasn't worried about them attacking him.

Mary Stegall invited all the men to stay, but she informed them that they would have to share the lone bed in the loft. The three men agreed that the arrangement was suitable, and they all went up to the loft and squeezed into the bed. Love, still not realizing he was in mortal jeopardy, fell asleep quickly.

Love's snoring was so loud that the Harpes could not get to sleep. One of them decided that he had to silence the sleeping man. Taking the tomahawk he always carried in his belt, the murderer raised the weapon as high as he could and then brought it down on Love's head with as much force as he could muster. Love's skull broke open and his brains squirted out onto the bed.

The gory scene of the dead man covered with blood leaking out from his split skull did not bother the Harpes. Both men went to sleep in short order and slept until just before dawn.

Upon waking, the men climbed down out of the loft and went into the main house. They complained to Mrs. Stegall about Love's snoring, but did not tell her they had murdered him. She assumed that the exhausted surveyor was still in bed sleeping.

The Harpes told Mrs. Stegall that they were hungry and asked her to prepare a hot breakfast for them. She was happy to cook for the two head bashers, but she told them that her son was sick and she had to attend to him first. That being the case, breakfast would have to wait for a considerable amount of time.

The Harpes didn't want their meal delayed. They offered to rock the baby in its cradle while she cooked them breakfast. Oddly unconcerned about putting her baby in the care of two men she knew were savage murderers, Mrs. Stegall agreed to the proposal.

In a matter of minutes, the baby stopped whimpering. The hospitable woman prepared the meal and called the men to sit and eat. Mary Stegall was amazed that her son had remained so quiet for so long, and she went to check on him while the men enjoyed their hot breakfast. The woman came up to the crib and looked into it. What she saw was shocking beyond description.

Mary Stegall had expected her innocent little one to be slumbering quietly. Instead, she saw the baby virtually floating in a puddle of its own blood, his throat slashed from ear to ear, his empty eyes staring at the ceiling, and he was cold, dead.

The woman screeched in horror and fell to the floor in despair. The villains, not wishing her wailing to spoil their breakfast, put a stop to it. They grabbed Mrs. Stegall's butcher knives, one of them the same knife they used to murder the baby. They picked up the distraught woman and plunged the knives into her several times. Then they let her fall and bleed out on the floor. After stabbing Mary Stegall, the murderers returned to the table and finished eating.

Neville Lindsay later testified to the brutality of the killing. "Three case-knives were stuck into the body of Mrs. Stegall, one of them was buried in so deep that the fire which consumed the house would not burn the handle."

After breakfast, the Harpes rummaged through the house and took everything of value they could carry – including Major Love's hat – and then they set the structure ablaze. In a short time, a hellish inferno engulfed the house.

Before leaving the despoiled and destroyed Stegall homestead, the Harpes took Major Love's mare and another horse belonging to Moses Stegall. They rode a ways from the scene of their latest crime and hid themselves just off the road between Stegall's farm and McBee's home. There they awaited their expected prey.

The Harpes believed that Squire McBee would see the smoke coming from the Stegall house and would rush toward the place to help extinguish the blaze. The Harpes expected that when McBee rode near them, they would spring out and murder him before he had the chance to react.

McBee was not the first person that came down the road. Two men, one named Hudgens and the other Gilmore, had been to Robertson's Lick to get a supply of salt, and they, with their two dogs, were walking back home with it. Thinking Hudgens and Gilmore may have spotted them, the Harpes, brandishing their rifles, came out from their hiding place, stopping the two men. The Harpes accused the two of murdering the Stegall family and of burning down the house. Hudgens and Gilmore were incredulous when told they were under arrest, and they denied the ridiculous charges.

The Harpes, once again playing a role perfectly, told their prisoners that they had to appear before Justice of the Peace Silas McBee and prove their innocence. Hudgens and Gilmore, certain that they could prove the arrest was a case of mistaken identity, willingly submitted to arrest and agreed to go to McBee's house where they could straighten out the matter quickly and be on their way with their salt.

The Harpes rode behind as the prisoners walked along for just a few strides when Micajah Harpe raised his rifle and fired. The rifle ball struck Gilmore in the back of the head, and the man was dead before he hit the ground face first. Hudgens, seeing his companion murdered, tried to escape into the woods and get away from the horror, but before he could, Wiley Harpe rode up to him and beat the poor man's brains out with his rifle butt.

The Harpes did not kill the two dogs belonging to Hudgens and Gilmore. Perhaps because of their encounter with McBee's hounds, they decided to keep these dogs as their own.

The murderers moved the bodies of Hudgens and Gilmore off the path, went back into hiding, and waited patiently for Silas McBee to come down the road. The wait proved to be in vain.

At about the same time the Harpe brothers were committing their latest murders, John Pyles and four others from Christian County, Kentucky, were returning from Robertson's Lick on a different path than the one the Harpes guarded. Pyles and his men rode upon the remnants of the Stegall house and found there was nothing salvageable. Pyles looked around and, seeing no one, felt it prudent to report the fire to someone with authority. Pyles and his companions took the path the Harpes guarded towards McBee's home to notify him of the fire.

On their way to the McBee farm, Pyles and the four others rode past the well-hidden Harpes without seeing the murderers. The Harpes let the men ride on without taking any action, reasoning that the five men would bring McBee back with them. When they did, the Harpes intended to give ambush and slaughter their original target, as well as Pyles and the other men.

Squire McBee had not noticed smoke coming from the Stegall home and didn't know anything about it until John Pyles reported it to him. McBee immediately grabbed his best gun, saddled his horse, and rode to William Grissom's cabin about a mile north of Stegall's. Luckily, instead of taking the road where the Harpes waited to spring an ambush, the Squire took a shorter route on a less travelled path,

After a few minutes of conversation, McBee asked Grissom to come with him to the Stegall homestead. Grissom and several of his family members armed themselves and rode to the burned house. Upon arrival, they found the smoldering ruins of the home as Pyles described, as well as the three charred bodies. Because of the condition of the victims, they buried all three beside the house.

With their grim task complete, the party rode to McBee's home along the same shortcut he'd taken earlier. Again, McBee's choice of route thwarted the Harpes and likely saved the Squire's life.

McBee's party went into his house and began planning the creation of a posse to track down the Harpes. While this was happening, Moses Stegall rode up and McBee delivered the horrible news to him. McBee asked the distraught man if he would ride to Robertson's Lick and try to round up some volunteers to join the pursuit party. Stegall wanted the Harpes dead, and although he felt a temptation to go after them alone, he finally agreed to McBee's request.

The Harpes waited until the afternoon before they abandoned their vigil and went back to the hideout where their wives were. Then they went on the run again with their women, their children, a stock of supplies, and their horses.

Matthew Christian stated that immediately after Stegall came to Robertson's Lick with news of the murder, he made for Stegall's farm, and what he saw there convinced him that "the report with all its terrible details was true." Christian continued that from Stegall's, he and the other volunteers from Robertson's Lick went to William Grissom's home.

The volunteers were unaware that Grissom's family had already departed and gone to McBee's place, where they intended to stay until the posse returned from the pursuit. At the vacated house, posse members found a note tacked to the front door. The note, addressed to Moses Stegall and signed with Silas Magby's name, stated, "Come to my house without delay." A jacket that the men presumed belonged to Major William Love hung on the door beside the note.

Believing that Magby had information that would aid in the capture of the Harpe brothers, Stegall, John Leiper, Neville Lindsey, and Matthew Christian started immediately for the Magby farm. As they rode along, someone hidden in the brush alongside the road fired a weapon at the party. The bullet didn't hit anyone, and the soon-to-be pursuers believed that one of the Harpes shot at them.

The men discovered that Magby had not been to Grissom's farm that day, and that he had written no note to Stegall. The forged note, coupled with the fact that the Harpes had already begun their flight from the area, is proof positive that the murderers had allies. In fact, everywhere the Harpes went, they enlisted others to help them. In this case, the Harpes prearranged the attempted ambush with an accomplice before they went back on the run. No one ever discovered the identity of the person that hid in the bushes and tried to waylay Stegall.

After surviving the murder attempt, the posse members returned to Grissom's place and spent the night.

The next morning, Stegall returned to McBee's house with Leiper, Christian, and Lindsey. These four joined Silas McBee, William Grissom, and James Tompkins, and formed a posse of seven. They promised to do whatever necessary to capture the Harpes, including dying for their cause, if need be.

McBee and his pursuit party located the best mounts that could get, armed themselves, and gathered enough provisions to last a few days. Around noontime, they began their quest. They didn't know they were almost a full day behind the Harpes.

McBee and the others were sure they knew where their adversaries were, and they feared the ruffians might double back and attack their defenseless family members. To avoid an attack, those posse members with families left them at McBee's house, along with a slave and a few guns for added protection.

The posse located the Harpe trail quickly and followed it to the south for a few miles. Then they came upon a place with disrupted vegetation and trampled-down grass. McBee reasoned that the outlaws had stampeded a herd of buffalo across the path in order to make it impossible to track them. Having discerned the Harpes' strategy, McBee and his men relocated the trail of the outlaws quickly. After that, they never lost it again.

Just before nightfall, McBee and his men stopped and made camp on the western shore of Pond River. They hobbled their horses and, not wanting to alert the outlaws by making a fire, they ate a cold supper before they made their beds on the ground. They considered the possibility that the Harpes would double back and launch an attack against them, but they did not post a guard. No attack came, but during the night, a brief rain shower added to their general discomfort.

At daybreak on this humid morning, McBee's men broke camp, crossed Pond River at a shallow point, and picked up the trail of the outlaws again. The posse moved quickly and easily, and about an hour after breaking camp, came upon the bodies of the dogs belonging to the recently murdered Hudgens and Gilmore. Apparently, the Harpes had killed the animals to keep them from barking and giving away their position. In fact, the murdered dogs provided the posse with valuable clues.

The temperature during August 1799 had been unusually hot, sometimes bordering on unbearable. When posse members viewed the dogs, they saw the animals displayed no sign of swelling or decomposition. This proved that the dogs had not been dead for very long, and that the fugitives were not far ahead of them.

A man with military experience, McBee understood that his horses might make noise and alert the Harpes. He ordered his four best men (Leiper, Stegall, Christian, and Lindsay) to dismount and go ahead on foot as quickly and as quietly as they could. In the meantime, McBee, Grissom, and Tompkins followed behind with the horses. McBee and the other two stayed close enough to the four men in the lead to rush in to reinforce them if a gun battle ensued, but far enough behind to maintain adequate noise discipline.

The four men forging forward in the unknown were tense. They believed they would encounter the Harpes and engage in a life or death confrontation at any moment, but they did not. After about a mile, McBee decided the Harpes were not as close as he had thought. He saw no need to tire the four men unnecessarily and he ordered them to remount. Then the posse continued along together on horseback.

The good luck the Harpes had always seemed to experience could not continue forever, and on this day, it finally failed them. As McBee's avengers went along, they saw their quarry on a hillside a considerable distance from them.

The Harpes, holding their rifles, were with another man. Micajah Harpe was holding his horse by its bridle, but Wiley Harpe didn't have a horse with him. The murderers were speaking with another man whom they had just encountered. This man, whom McBee didn't recognize, also held a weapon. Another thing the pursuers did not know was that the man talking to the Harpes had unwittingly saved the lives of the two remaining Harpe children and one of the Harpe women.

After the Harpes had failed to ambush McBee, they rode to the hideout where their wives waited. After spending the night, Micajah Harpe was in a hurry to leave for safer territory. He was certain that in a very short time, a posse would be nipping at their heels. He also wanted to move as quickly as possible, and he viewed the little children as an unnecessary encumbrance. He informed Wiley and the three women that he planned to kill the babies, discard their bodies, and leave the area before noon.

There was some debate, but the others did not dare argue too much with Micajah Harpe. As always, he was the dominant person in the group, and the other adults bent to his will. They agreed to sacrifice the children for the sake of the monsters.

Sally Harpe's soul was not completely black. She couldn't simply hand her child over for the slaughter. If her husband Wiley would not do anything to help the child, she would. Sally took the little one to an area beside a small stream and placed it under a shelving rock that jutted out from the hillside. She then placed herself on the ground in front of the rock, blocking her baby from view. She knew she could not protect her child from murder, but she was determined to die with the little one.

Sally waited for a short time, and then Wiley came up to her and told her it was time to put their baby to death. Before Wiley could act, he noticed George Smith approaching. Smith was a "horse hunter" by trade. That is, he rounded up wild horses (and strays as well) and sold them to other settlers. Sensing danger, Wiley Harpe alerted his brother, and Micajah Harpe jumped on Major Love's mare and rode to where the other men stood. Within minutes, the posse arrived.

Seeing the Harpes excited McBee. No longer worrying about alerting the outlaws, he yelled, "There they are!" He then spurred his horse and rode across the level strip of land separating his position from the hillside where the Harpes stood as quickly as he could.

The Harpes heard the commotion McBee caused and attempted to make their escape. Micajah Harpe immediately mounted his horse and sped off in one direction while Wiley ran as fast as he could the other way. Of course, there was no time now to murder the children.

Evidently bewildered, the man speaking with the Harpes ran towards McBee. When he was sixty to eighty yards from the hard riding Squire, he tried to hunker down behind a tree.

Thinking the man was about to use the tree to steady his aim before shooting, McBee raised his weapon, loaded with two balls and "blasted away." A result of luck more than marksmanship, both balls struck the man – one in the right thigh and the other in the right arm.

The other posse members raised their weapons as well, and were about to finish off the wounded man as he squirmed on the ground in pain. Then Moses Stegall, who was riding near McBee, suddenly recognized the wounded man as a settler that lived about three miles away on Pond River. Wishing to save the life of the innocent man, Stegall yelled out, "Don't shoot, it's George Smith!" With that, the men lowered their weapons.

Smith recognized McBee and called him by name. In an odd twist, the wounded man admitted that he had intended to open fire on McBee, and then he asked forgiveness for it. Smith explained that he was almost out of his mind from fear that the Harpes would murder him at any moment. Then when the commotion started, he wasn't thinking straight, and he perceived McBee as a threat. Smith claimed that he was only trying to protect himself.

Smith continued that this morning he left his home carrying a kettle, intending to fill it in a nearby stream. As always, when he ventured out alone in this troubled land, he carried his weapon with him that morning. On his return trip home, Wiley Harpe suddenly appeared. The younger Harpe brother asked Smith about the settlements nearby. Wiley's tone was harsh and Smith noticed that the stranger was speaking loudly. Smith did not know that the Harpe camp was only about one-quarter mile away, but he was certain that Wiley was attempting draw the attention of another.

Hearing his brother, Micajah Harpe jumped on a horse and rode to where Wiley and the intimidated Smith stood. Micajah slid from his mount and stood between Smith and Wiley. Smith knew the Harpes intended to kill him, but his fear froze him and he couldn't do anything. Thankfully for him, the McBee search party arrived before the Harpes could slaughter Smith and dispose of his carcass.

Smith's wounds were not life threatening, but he said he could use help getting back home. McBee promised to help the man, but not until the posse had captured or killed the Harpes. The Squire and his men rode alone, leaving George Smith there to await their return. McBee never came back to aid the man he had wrongly wounded. After he gave up on the posse returning, "Smith hobbled home by himself."

After surviving yet another near miss, Micajah Harpe did not go directly back to camp. He feared that the posse had taken it before they caught up with him and had posted guards there. He did not re-enter the stronghold until he was certain that it was safe to do so. Unable to think about anything except getting away, Micajah Harpe abandoned his plan of murdering the children.

When the Harpes scattered, Sally took her little one and returned to camp as quickly as she could. Soon, she and both Harpe children were left alone at the hideout.

It didn't take the pursers long to locate the Harpe camp – which was something of a natural fortress. The camp was just a few steps from the road leading to "Free Henry" Ford. Still, it concealed the outlaws well. The stronghold was a space about fifteen feet square, situated under a shelving rock that jutted from the cliff of a ridge facing to the south. Directly in front of the living area, a large rock secluded it and left nothing but a narrow space for an entrance. In all, the easily defensible hideout offered the outlaws excellent safety from attack.

The seven men approached the camp with trepidation. They expected an intense gunfight with the Harpes. When they entered the dark hole, they found that Wiley Harpe's wife, Sally, was the only adult there. When McBee questioned her, she said Micajah Harpe had just been there, and that he had loaded each of his women on a fresh horse and rode away with them in haste. She also seemed more than happy to tell McBee which direction Micajah Harpe and his women rode.

McBee and his men gave chase, but they couldn't find Micajah Harpe's trail. Thinking the woman had deceived him to give Micajah Harpe extra time to escape, an infuriated McBee wheeled his horse around and went back to the Harpe hideout. Upon his return, the angry Squire lifted his gun and threatened to blow Sally's brains out if she didn't tell him the true path Micajah Harpe traveled away from camp. Protesting that she had not lied, she pointed out the direction Micajah Harpe had taken for a second time.

This time, convinced that Sally Harpe was telling the truth, the posse set off again, hoping to make up the thirty minutes they had lost by overlooking Micajah Harpe's tracks before. The delay notwithstanding, McBee and his troop were in high spirits. They felt confident that they would soon catch up to Harpe and his women, and then kill or capture the monstrous murderer.

McBee didn't lead his posse, however. He intended to bring Sally Harpe to justice too. The Squire loaded her upon one of the horses Micajah Harpe had left behind, and they followed the others. McBee and Sally didn't fall too far behind the others, however.

Only about two miles from the camp, the party saw Micajah Harpe and his wives on a ridge a short distance ahead of them. One of the posse members yelled for Harpe to stop and surrender. Of course, he did not. Instead, he spurred his horse, and being the coward he was, he abandoned the women, as he made a mad dash to escape his pursuers. John Leiper fired at Harpe, but his bullet missed its mark.

The posse arrested the Harpe women, and James Tompkins and Neville Lindsey took them in tow. Meanwhile, Leiper, Matthew Christian, William Grissom, and Moses Stegall continued the chase as quickly as the uneven terrain allowed.

Micajah Harpe rode his horse as hard as he could, but he couldn't shake his pursuers. Christian, Stegall, and Grissom each fired at Harpe, but only Christian hit the fleeing outlaw. The bullet struck the villain in the leg. The criminal, now wounded, unable to break free from the posse, and his rifle in need of reloading, felt he had to take a desperate chance.

Seeing that Leiper had moved a considerable distance in front of the other pursuers, and believing Leiper's weapon was empty too, Harpe gambled. Harpe pulled back the reins and stopped his horse. Then he dismounted, turned his back to the rider, and began to prime his rifle. Micajah Harpe thought he would have his rifle reloaded before the fast galloping Leiper could get to him. Once ready, Harpe would kill his adversary, remount, and ride away.

In another strange twist, the rain the night before had gotten Leiper's gunpowder wet and had made his rifle inoperable. Since Leiper was the best shot among the group and Tompkins seldom found his target, the two swapped rifles before they broke camp that morning. The swap included the gunpowder Micajah Harpe had loaned Tompkins. Ironically, had Micajah Harpe not loaned Tompkins dry gunpowder, the outlaw's plan would have succeeded.

As it was, Micajah Harpe had miscalculated. The gun Leiper had borrowed from Tompkins was ready to fire. Leiper took careful aim and squeezed the trigger. There was a loud report as the molten lead ball exited the rifle barrel.

The projectile flew true and struck the massive criminal midway of his back, near his spine.

A weaker man would have fallen to the ground and lost consciousness – not so Micajah Harpe. He turned and faced his shooter. Then he leveled his gun at Leiper and pulled his trigger. Harpe must have felt a sinking feeling inside when the hammer fell, but other than making a clicking sound, nothing happened. Harpe, his notorious luck played out, threw down his useless rifle, and pulled his tomahawk from his rawhide belt. He couldn't use it, however, because his pursuers were too far away.

By the time Harpe's weapon misfired, Christian had come alongside Leiper, with Stegall and Grissom trailing behind. Harpe knew he was in no condition to fight with more than one enemy, and he decided to climb back aboard his hot and tired horse and try to escape. Yet no matter how hard he urged the exhausted animal on, he could not put any extra space between him and those chasing him. In fact, Leiper and Christian made up ground quickly.

As they chased behind the bleeding criminal, Leiper and Christian yelled out to Harpe to stop. Showing his defiance, he answered their commands by raising his tomahawk and shaking it at the men closing in on him. Finally, Harpe decided to gamble again. He yelled back that if Leiper and Christian would stop their horses, then he would surrender.

Happy that the chase was finally ending, the two pursuers stopped their gasping horses and dismounted. Knowing they could not trust Harpe to give up without a fight, Leiper and Christian began loading their weapons. Thinking he might gain an advantage yet, Harpe threw his tomahawk at Leiper, applied sharp spur to tender flank, and bolted away on his jaded steed.

Leiper was using both hands to load his rifle and didn't bother to hold his horse. Harpe's tomahawk spooked Leiper's animal, and it sprinted in the direction of the fleeing felon. Christian jumped on his horse, rode after, and caught Leiper's animal. Then, he brought it back to his ally. Falling behind Harpe again, Christian and Leiper resumed the chase hurriedly, without finishing the reloading of their rifles.

The pursuers picked up Harpe's trail minutes later and followed it for another half a mile. Then they rode through a thick, but easily manageable canebrake, about two miles from the Unity Baptist Church, and caught up with the fugitive just as he was exiting it. The spent horse walked along slowly and Harpe, weak from the loss of blood, could barely remain in the saddle. The victorious pursuers pulled the unarmed outlaw from his horse, and he fell to the ground with a thud, landing under a large oak tree. Micajah Harpe knew he was beaten, and he was finished resisting.

Thus, the posse finally had the scoundrel that had terrorized so many for so long under their control. He was now helpless, and as he remained prostrate on the ground, begged for a drink of water. Leiper pulled a moccasin from one of the outlaw's dirty feet, walked the one hundred yards or so to the Pond River, filled the shoe, and brought it back to Harpe. The dying man swallowed as much of the water as he could get down.

Had McBee and his men not hated the wonton killer so much, they may have pitied him. Of course, they did not. They felt his suffering was just reward for all the suffering he had wrought on others. Regardless of their feelings, this creature, once so feared, was slowly dying – too slowly. McBee didn't want to spend too much time waiting for Micajah Harpe to expire. He told the prisoner that there was no chance of survival, and that a member of the posse would soon finish him.

Yet, McBee still desired to exhibit a degree of compassion. The Squire said Harpe could have time to pray and make "preparation for another world." Harpe seemed unconcerned about the afterlife, and he didn't reply to McBee regarding heaven and hell.

The big man did want to talk to his wife Susan. He asked Christian to bring her forward so he could tell her he "wished her to do better in the future." Micajah Harpe also said he wanted to "acquaint her with one thing that was hid." Christian did not bring Susan to Harpe. She was a distance away from the outlaw's death scene with Tompkins and Lindsay.

There were persistent rumors that the Harpe brothers had hidden a portion of the gold they had stolen from their victims. Harpe's mention of "one thing that was hid" intrigued Silas

McBee. McBee asked Harpe if the rumors of hidden gold were correct. Harpe, perhaps hoping that McBee would delay killing him, said they were.

Harpe told the Squire he had hidden two saddlebags loaded with gold in the woods near Pond River. When asked the exact location of the saddlebags, the outlaw said McBee could find them alongside a stream that branched easterly from the river, about twenty miles from its mouth. Harpe's description disappointed McBee. The Justice of the Peace knew the area around Pond River well and he knew there was no tributary such as the murderer described. Despite legends about the Harpe gold, no one ever found any.

Moses Stegall, as one can imagine, wanted Micajah Harpe dead as quickly as possible. He pulled his knife from its belt sheath and waved the sharp blade in Harpe's face. Stegall said he intended to sever the outlaw's head in retribution for the murder of his wife and son.

Harpe, resting on his right side in a puddle of his own blood, responded to Stegall by trying to gain pity on one hand, and blaming another for his crimes on the other. Harpe said, "I am but a young man, but young as I am, I feel the death-damp [the cold, clammy sweat which sometimes precedes death] already upon my brow."

Perhaps trying to prolong his life for a few moments, Harpe proceeded to confess to some of his murders. He gave vivid details of between twenty and thirty of the killings he had committed. Of course, we know now that the number he killed was much greater than he admitted. Yet, the only murder he expressed any remorse about committing was that of his little daughter.

Then, his voice growing fainter with every word, Harpe again tried to place blame on another. He told his captors, "Before I die I could wish that old Baldwin might be brought here, as he is the man who instigated me to the commission of all my crimes."

The man called Baldwin was under constant suspicion of criminal activity. He lived at a place called Green Tree Grove in present-day Caldwell County, Kentucky. Eventually, authorities brought Baldwin to trial, but unable to produce adequate evidence against him, the court acquitted him.

The posse members rested for about an hour while they waited for Harpe to die, but he wouldn't accommodate them. Stegall finally lost his patience and decided to put an end to Harpe. Stegall pointed his gun at the criminal's head and took aim. Harpe, still unwilling to die, bobbed his head left and right trying to avoid the rifle ball. Unable to target Harpe's skull for a kill shot, Stegall said to McBee, "Very well, I believe I will not upon reflection shoot him in the head, for I want to preserve that as a trophy."

Then Stegall fired at Harpe's body, and the ball struck him in the left side. The villain did not make another sound as the remainder of his blood gushed out and his life force ebbed away. In a matter of seconds, the murdering marauder was dead.

Intent on getting his trophy before Harpe stopped breathing, Stegall pulled out his knife with one hand, grabbed the outlaw's greasy hair with the other, and severed Harpe's head from its body. After admiring his handiwork for a bit, Stegall held the head up for all to see.

Stegall realized suddenly that he needed a way to carry the head with him. Squire McBee had with him saddlebags in which he had carried provisions for the pursuit. He volunteered to loan them to the decapitator. Stegall removed everything from one of the bags, and put what he could into the other. Then he stuffed Harpe's head into the empty bag. His hands, still bloody from the performance of his gruesome task, Stegall slung the saddlebags across his horse, and he and the victorious posse rode away from the scene.

McBee and the others thought so little of Micajah Harpe that they didn't bother to bury his headless body. Instead, they left what was left of him there in the wilderness of Muhlenberg County where he died. Soon insects, wild beasts, and vultures had their way with the "the terror of the west."

McBee and the others located Tompkins and Lindsay, who were looking after Harpe's wives. The Squire informed the women of the death of the scoundrel. If Micajah Harpe's wives mourned for him, or displayed any emotion at all, none of those that witnessed his demise ever mentioned it. In fact, it appears that the women displayed indifference toward Micajah Harpe's death.

After the whole posse reunited, they rode back to the Harpe hideout. If they hoped to find Wiley Harpe there, they were disappointed. They searched the place and found no money beyond a dollar and a half in coins. They did locate the nine stolen horses at the Harpe camp and returned them, along with the animal Micajah Harpe rode, to their owners. Unfortunately, the ordeal Harpe put it through ruined his mount, and soon after McBee returned it to Major Love's wife, it died.

The triumphant posse, carrying Harpe's head with them, began the thirty-five mile trek to Robertson's Lick. The men and their captives moved along until near nightfall, when they decided to make camp. Realizing they didn't have enough food left for everyone, they stopped at a field along the road and pulled enough ripe corn for their supper. Having no other means of carrying the corn, Stegall pushed the unhusked ears into the bag with Harpe's head. Later, when they pulled the blood-soaked corn out of the bag and roasted it, one of the more squeamish men refused to eat "because it had been put into the bag with Harpe's head."

At some point Stegall removed Harpe's head from the saddlebag and forced the dead outlaw's wife, Susan, to carry it for a distance. As she walked, she slung the head back and forth like an Easter basket, muttering, "Damn this head."

The party brought the villain's head to a crossroads about half a mile from Robertson's Lick, not far from where Harpe committed his final murder. There, they displayed the head as a hideous and horrifying reminder to outlaws that they could expect the same from the good folk there. They erected the grisly exhibit on the side of the highway about three miles north of what became the town of Dixon, at the crossroads running south of Henderson, Kentucky, going in one direction to Marion and Eddyville, and in the other direction to Madison and Russellville.

Several accounts of how the posse displayed the head exist. Some say Stegall lodged Harpe's head "in the forks of a tree" or "stuck on the sharpened end of the limb of a tree." Others contend that he affixed it "upon the top of a lofty pole." Still another report relates, "A tall young tree growing by the side of the trail or road, was selected and trimmed of its branches to its top, and then made sharp. On this point the head was fashioned."

Regardless as to exactly how Stegall's trophy graced the roadside, it remained hanging there for a considerable period. An eyewitness account states, "The skull and jaw-bones remained there for many years – after all else had been decomposed and mingled with the dust."

The place where Stegall wedged the head gained the name "Harpe's Head." And the thoroughfare that went past it, between the Deer Creek community and Robertson's Lick, earned the name of Harpe's Head Road.

Many legends about Micajah Harpe's head arose. One of the most interesting was that several years after Stegall placed Harpe's head in the tree, an old woman in the neighborhood had a relative that suffered from "fits." She heard that a human skull beaten into powder and mixed with certain other ingredients would, when ingested by a person subject to seizures, result in a miraculous cure. Armed with that knowledge, she retrieved Harpe's skull and mixed her concoction. There is no information whether or not the "medicine" worked the hoped-for miracle.

12. The Harpe Women

WITH one of the bloody brothers dead and the other on the run, the only people left to stand trial were the Harpe women. So for the second time, they went before a judge, charged with the crimes committed by their husbands.

After mounting the disembodied head of Micajah Harpe, the posse took their female captives another twenty miles or so to Henderson County. Once there, they took their prisoners to "the little log dungeon, then located on the river bank" and turned them over to the authorities.

On September 4, 1799, about a week after their incarceration, the Henderson County sheriff took the women to the courthouse, to stand before the Court of Quarter and answer the charges brought against them. Judges Samuel Hopkins and Abraham Landers presided over the hearing.

The chief judge, Samuel Hopkins was a man of standing. Although he was only 46, he had experienced a great deal. Born in Virginia, he served on the Staff of General Washington during the American Revolution, eventually rising to the rank of Colonel. He moved to Kentucky in 1796, studied law, and became an attorney. Hopkins had seen his share of blood and guts, but nothing like what the Harpes had done.

Later, after giving up his judgeship, Hopkins served in the Kentucky legislature and State Senate. When the War of 1812 began, Hopkins accepted appointment of Major General and served as commander-in-chief of the western frontier (Illinois and Indiana Territory). Hopkins continued to live in Henderson County until his death in 1819.

The court charged all three women with "being parties in the murder of Mary Stegall, James Stegall an infant, and William Love at the house of Moses Stegall in this County and in burning his house and robbing and stealing the horses, goods and effects of the said Moses Stegall on the night of the 20th day of August last."

The women had been through this type of ordeal before, and court proceedings didn't intimidate them anymore. They denied any guilt.

The judges then called, one after the other, John Leiper, Neville Lindsey, Matthew Christian, and Isom Sellers to testify. This narrative has already related the events to which they testified.

The judges also gave the Harpe women an opportunity to defend themselves. They again denied any wrongdoing, but they didn't say anything tending to prove their innocence.

Indicting the women was an easy decision for the judges to make. They ordered the women and babies transported to the jail at Russellville. The next date for trial in the District Court was October 28, and the Harpe women found themselves at the top of the docket.

On September 6, the Sheriff and five guards began escorting the Harpe women and children the ninety-five miles to the Logan County jail. Upon arrival, they turned the prisoners over to Logan County Sheriff Major William Stewart. Stewart had pursued the Harpe brothers several times, but his pursuits had resembled a dog chasing its own tail, and he had never gotten close to them. Despite his embarrassing failures at bringing the criminals to justice, and his revulsion at the many outrages the Harpes committed, Stewart was a fair man.

Sheriff Stewart treated the women with a degree of compassion which they had seldom experienced before. When Stewart took custody of the Harpe women they were "coarse, sunburnt, and wretchedly attired," and infested with lice.

Later, Sheriff Stewart described the women briefly. Susan, Micajah Harpe's first wife, was "rather tall, rawboned, dark hair and eyes, and rather ugly," and about twenty-five years old. Betsey was "rather handsome, light hair and blue eyes and a perfect contrast with her sister." Sally, the wife of Little Harpe, was "really pretty and delicate." There is no certainty about the ages of the women, but most observers guessed them to be younger than they actually were.

Stewart told the women that if they would promise not to attempt an escape, he would not keep them locked in cells. The prisoners readily agreed. Some wondered why the sheriff would risk his career gambling that the Harpe women would not attempt to run away. However, Stewart felt he was a good judge of character, and was willing to take responsibility for his actions.

Major Stewart did not stop at allowing the women a degree of liberty. He also went around the community and collected a few articles of clothing for them. He had the women and children cleaned up and lodged in the courthouse, which was more sanitary than the jail. Stewart then brought in two spinning wheels and put the women to work.

Legends arose that the hatred for the Harpe women was so great that members of the community threatened to tear down the log jail and lynch the prisoners. The stories continued that in order to protect them, Sheriff Stewart moved the women to a hiding place in the country, and kept them there until it was time for their trial. There is no documented evidence proving the validity of these legends, but there was a considerable amount of hostility in Russellville expressed regarding the Harpe women.

It is true that Moses Stegall and a number of his friends rode to Russellville, intending to kill the three Harpe women if a jury acquitted them. Evidence against them notwithstanding, the Harpe women had won in court before, and Stegall promised to prevent them from escaping justice again.

Learning of Stegall's designs, Sheriff Stewart withdrew the trustee status from the women and returned them to the jail. Stewart didn't admit he was protecting the prisoners. Instead, he stated, "it would never do to turn such characters loose upon society."

Finally, concerned that Stegall and his party would storm the jail, Stewart moved the women from the jail in the middle of the night. He took them to a large cave about five miles from town and sheltered them there. Stegall lost interest in exacting revenge, and in a few days, he returned home. Satisfied Stegall was gone, the Sheriff brought the oft-moved Harpe women back to town.

The women came before the District Court on October 28. By law, three judges were supposed to preside over the case, but Judges Samuel McDowell and John Allen were unable to attend the sessions. The women could have demanded a delay, but they wanted the trial to proceed as quickly as possible. They agreed to have Judge James G. Hunter preside alone.

The attorney assigned to defend the women was twenty-two year old boy genius, Felix Grundy. Grundy was in his first year of practicing law, but he had already exhibited some of the brilliance that eventually made him an important national figure. He later served in the Kentucky legislature, and as Chief Justice of the Kentucky Supreme Court. Then, after relocating to Tennessee, Grundy served in the Congress, the US Senate, and as Attorney General of the United States.

Each of the Harpe women stood trial on her own in front of different juries. Susan Harpe stood trial on October 29, and the other two trials took place the next day. None of the juries were willing to bring in a guilty verdict, and each of them returned a verdict of "Not Guilty." While some members of the community disagreed with the verdicts, no one attempted to molest the Harpe women after the court freed them.

Sheriff Stewart gained the confidence of the women in his custody, and they spoke to him freely. Stewart's main interest was in learning why the Harpes committed so many brutal and senseless crimes. The women told Major Stewart that once in Knoxville, authorities had arrested and jailed the Harpe men unjustly. Upon their release, the Harpes "declared war against all mankind, and determined to murder and rob until they were killed."

The excuse that the Harpes became serial killers because the authorities in Knoxville abused them is false. The Harpe men were active criminals when they crossed the mountains into Tennessee and they killed several people before they arrived in Knoxville. Their brutality did escalate over time, but there is no evidence that any jail term pushed them over the edge.

The three women that rode the "hurricane of all horrors" for so long received much criticism in the 19th Century for their association with the bloody brothers. But after they were finally free, at least two of them lived better lives.

Betsey Harpe, finally freed from the clutches of Micajah Harpe, married John Hufstetter. The two rented a place on Colonel Anthony Butler's plantation about six miles south of

Russellville, where they scratched out a living as sharecroppers. Betsey made additional income by raising chickens for Mrs. Butler. Later, the Hufstetters moved to a place on the Red River in Tennessee, and still later to a place on the Duck River. Betsey's son, calling himself "Joe Roberts," lived to adulthood and enlisted in the American Army.

Susan Harpe did not remarry. She also moved into a cabin on Colonel Butler's plantation. She reared a child named Lovey as her own. However, the evidence indicates that Micajah Harpe killed Susan's daughter, and that this child was actually the daughter of Sally Harpe. Regardless, Susan accepted Lovey as her own child.

Lovey Harpe was very pretty, of average size, with raven hair, a dark complexion, and dark eyes. Because of her intoxicating beauty, suitors were always desirous to court her, but she kept most of them at a distance.

Not surprisingly, considering Lovey Harp's beginnings, she did poorly in school. It wasn't that she lacked intelligence; it was that she was a constant disruption. Lovey had a violent temper and she was "always pouting and angry." Most of her classmates avoided her.

Both Susan and Lovey had a reputation of having bad characters, and they became outcasts. They could not overcome their previous association with the Harpes. Lovey Harpe's antisocial behavior caused intense animosity against her, in and around Russellville. Leaders forced the mother and daughter to leave.

Colonel Butler continued to show the Harpe women compassion. He owned a mill in Christian County near Pond River, and he invited Susan and Lovey Harpe to move into a cabin there. Susan died a short time later, and Lovey relocated with the Butler family first to Pearl, Mississippi, and then a while later to Texas.

Oddly, Susan Harpe continued to show affection for Micajah Harpe long after his death. She defended her husband by contending that Wiley Harpe was the greater of the two villains. She told one of her neighbors in Russellville, "Big Harpe said to Little Harpe that he thought they had better quit killing people and go to some backwoods country, for if they did not, he feared they would be detected and killed. Whereupon, Little Harpe flew into a passion, cursed his brother for a coward, and said if he ever talked that way again he would shoot him." She continued that Micajah Harpe was so frightened that "Some days before Big Harpe's death he fancied the ground continually trembling beneath his feet."

Despite Susan's contentions, Micajah Harpe was the dominant of the brothers. And Wiley Harpe, being a coward and a moral weakling, allowed his brother to bully him. In fact, he followed his older brother's orders without question. This subservience went as far as agreeing to allow Micajah to murder Wiley's child.

Sally Rice came from a good family, and everyone that knew her thought highly of her. She fell in love with and married Wiley Harpe before she knew what kind of man he was. Throughout her ordeal, Sally displayed more humanity than did the other Harpe women. She was even willing to risk death to try to protect her daughter.

At her second trial, Sally Harpe's father was in the courtroom. After her acquittal, instead of chastising her for her previous life, he welcomed her back into the family and offered to take her back to Knoxville with him. Parson Rice's prodigal daughter happily agreed.

In 1820, Parson Rice and his family, including Sally, her second husband, and their daughter, migrated to Illinois. It had been two decades since the posse separated Sally from the evil that blew across the countryside like a tornado, but she still felt ashamed. When she accidently met Sheriff Stewart just before she crossed the Ohio River, Sally "sat down and with her face in her hands, had a weeping spell."

13. McBee's Avengers

NOT surprisingly, the seven men that brought down Micajah Harpe returned home to a welcome reserved for heroes. Beyond the adulation they received from their peers, they received payment from the grateful Kentucky government. On December 16, 1799, the state legislature adopted "An Act directing the payment of money to John Leiper and others."

The bill stated that "Micajah Harpe, a notorious offender" was guilty of "the most unheard of murders" and the Governor had, on April 22, offered a reward of $300 for the apprehension of said Harpe."

The Act continued, "Sundry good citizens . . . were, while in the attempt to apprehend him, reduced to the necessity of slaying him" and that they deserved to receive the money promised by the Governor. The bill ordered that John Leiper receive $100 and that James Tompkins, Silas McBee, Mathew Christian, Moses Stegall, Neville Lindsey, and William Grissom divide the remainder equally.

The bill also provided that Alexander McFarland, John McFarland, Daniel McFarland, and Robert White split $150 for their services. As noted earlier, the Governor appointed them to take charge of the Harpe brothers if found "in any adjacent state." It seems hardly fair that the McFarland brothers and White each receive $37.50 when they did nothing to apprehend the brothers, while six of the men actually facing the Harpes only collected $33.33, but that is what happened.

Most of the seven who ended Micajah Harpe's terrible rampage did well in later life. James Tompkins and Matthew Christian remained in Henderson County where they lived long, prosperous lives.

About a decade after exacting justice on Micajah Harpe, William Grissom pulled up stakes and moved across the Ohio River into Illinois. There he established a large farm and became wealthy.

Neville Lindsay eventually pushed on to the west and aided in the development of that part of Tennessee.

Silas McBee relocated to Pontotoc County, Mississippi, and established a large plantation on vibrant and rich soil. At his death, McBee was among the richest men in the state.

Two members of the posse did not fare as well as the five mentioned above. John Leiper and Moses Stegall were the driving force behind the posse. If the two had not been so zestful in the pursuit of the Harpes, McBee and the others might have given up the chase, as so many others had before. Thus, Leiper and Stegall most likely prevented Micajah Harpe from escaping.

Yet to their surprise and chagrin, Leiper and Stegall fell under suspicion almost as quickly as they returned home. Soon locals linked their names to the deeds committed by the Harpes.

John Leiper certainly knew the Harpes before he joined the posse that killed the older of the two. It is also possible –even likely – that he was involved in some of their criminal dealings. One piece of circumstantial evidence is that when the Harpes murdered Colonel Daniel Trabue's teenage son "Leiper then resided in Adair County and knew the Trabue family well." Leiper likely lived near the man referred to as "Old Man Roberts." If so, he probably conversed with the Harpes there. He might even have had firsthand knowledge of the murder of the Trabue boy.

Soon after the Harpes came into the area, Leiper moved from Henderson County. Speculation was that Leiper departed his home because he feared they would seek vengeance on him for joining the posse seeking the killers of John Trabue. If so, he would not have been the first person to pull up stakes and slip off to parts unknown to escape the deadly anger of the Harpes.

Despite speculation, it seems that the Harpes and Leiper remained on good terms. Certainly, the Harpes did locate Leiper's new location. As noted earlier, the Harpe women stopped by Leiper's cabin and asked for directions to Stegall's farm. Had the Harpes been out to murder him, Leiper would not have calmly conversed with the Harpe women.

Leiper also encountered legal troubles not associated with the Harpes. On July 3, 1799, a Henderson County grand jury indicted him for "living in adultery with Ann L. Allen, from the 20th day of last May." In those days, a charge of adultery was a serious offense, but there is no evidence that Leiper ever received punishment in connection with the case.

Leiper became the most energetic of those pursuing the Harpes, but it did not begin that way. When first approached to join the posse by Moses Stegall, he hesitated. Leiper declared that he didn't have a horse fit for the chase. He said he couldn't possibly volunteer for the endeavor unless someone could procure Captain Robert Robertson's horse for him. After the others struck a deal with Robertson, Leiper agreed to join the search party.

While a part of the posse, Leiper made comments tending to indicate that he knew the Harpes intimately. He told his partners in the pursuit that when he saw either of the Harpes, he "would stick to the chase until he killed them or they killed him."

Then as Leiper and Christian closed in on Micajah Harpe, the big man yelled at Leiper, "I told you to stay back or I'd kill you!"

Leiper replied, "My business with you is for one or the other of us to be killed."

The local folk always expressed a degree of appreciation to Leiper for his part in ridding the community of the murderous cancer that had eaten at it for so long. Yet many, perhaps most, of his neighbors felt his motives in going after Harpe were impure. He never shook the aura of suspicion surrounding him. Leiper spent the remainder of his short time on earth as a friendless outcast. He died of "fever" on Friday, February 6, 1807.

At first, Moses Stegall took a place as the most admired of the returning heroes. He had lost his wife, his child, and his home. Yet, Providence had given him the singular opportunity to strike the mortal blow against the man that wronged him so. That was the general view at first. But the general feeling of goodwill did not last very long.

Before Stegall went on the quest to rid the country of the Harpe malignancy, the community saw him as an unsavory figure. None trusted Stegall, but no one could pin any specific crime on him. He avoided arrest and jail, but not the prying eyes of his neighbors.

The tragic loss of his home and family engendered compassion for Stegall. Then his heroic pursuit and dispatch of the murderer engendered some respect for him. Those two things dampened the suspicions of Stegall for a short time. Yet the suspicions flared up again.

The truth that Stegall knew the Harpes was impossible to hide for very long. He had known the Harpe men when he lived in Knoxville. Beyond that, the Harpe women had inquired about the location of Stegall's house days before the Harpe men went there and killed his family. Armed with that information, some wondered about Stegall's actions regarding the captured Micajah Harpe. First, he threatened Harpe with a knife, and then he shot the outlaw to death.

In the excited fever of the present, Stegall's companions felt Stegall justified in sending the murderer to the hereafter. Upon reflection, however, some began to wonder if Stegall's motives in taking the impetuous act were different than first supposed. Harpe, although dying, was still able to speak, and he had already implicated one person for his crime spree. Did Stegall fear that Harpe was about to implicate *him* in a crime? Was it possible that Stegall had killed the desperado to silence him?

Rumors spread that Stegall was a criminal associate of the Harpes. Worse than that, a story circulated that Stegall left his wife and child alone in his house after he hired the Harpes to kill them. This, according to the rumors, allowed the evil man to rid himself of his bothersome family while avoiding suspicion that he committed the crime. The theory was interesting, but never proven.

Stegall died even before John Leiper did. Stegall's death was violent and bloody. In 1806, Stegall seduced a young girl whose family lived on the Trade Water River in Kentucky. Stegall beguiled the youth and asked her to run away with him. Blinded by her infatuation and her craving for adventure, she consented. Stegall spirited away his young "bride" in the middle of the night, and she went unmissed until the morning. The eloping couple rode northwest to a house about ten miles from the Ohio River. Stegall and the girl evidently intended to live there permanently.

When they discovered her missing, the girl's father and three older brothers started out after the deluded girl to bring her home. The outraged men traced Stegall to the house where the supposed newlyweds lived.

It was after dark when the father and his sons saw Moses Stegall and a group of others sitting outside the house under a canopy. Stegall and the others talked by the yellow light of an oil lamp, unaware that the four angry men were nearby. After creeping silently forward until they came close, the four rushed up to Stegall and opened fire upon him from close range. Stegall died instantly, and no one else received any wounds. The father grabbed his disgraced daughter and dragged her away. Horrified, the others sitting under the canopy dove for safety, and none of them made any move to stop the abduction. Soon the girl was home and Stegall was in his grave.

14. Rejoining Samuel Mason

ONE of the bloody brothers was dead, but the other was still alive, well, and deadly. In a weird, demonic miracle, Wiley Harpe had escaped from McBee's avengers. It was strange that even though he was on foot while Micajah was on horseback, none of the posse went after Wiley. Instead, as previously noted, they went first to the Harpe hideout, and then rode after Micajah. It may be that the only reason none of McBee's posse spread out and looked for Wiley in the woods is that they considered him less important a catch than Micajah was.

Word of Micajah Harpe's death spread across Kentucky and Tennessee as quickly as sheet lightning spreads across the sky on a summer evening. Everyone from the hills, the towns, the backwoods, and the canebrakes felt relief that the larger of the monsters was gone. Yet when word of Wiley Harpe's death didn't follow, general nervousness again rose like a fever in the wintertime.

For his part, Wiley Harpe's phenomenal luck held once more. He had somehow escaped with his head on his shoulders, but barely. He, like the snake he was, needed a hole in which to slither. Eventually Wiley Harpe, alone and having to make his own decisions for the first time in his life, decided to see if Samuel Mason would allow him to rejoin his gang.

The entanglement of the lives of Wiley Harpe and Samuel Mason is so complete that it is impossible to tell the full story of Wiley Harpe without including a brief recounting of the life of Samuel Mason, the self-proclaimed "King of the River Pirates."

Samuel Ross Mason was born in 1739 in Norfolk, Virginia. He grew up in what is now Charles Town, West Virginia. Mason grew into "a man of gigantic stature and more than ordinary talents." His weight hovered well over 200 pounds, and "at any time in his life or in any situation, had something extremely ferocious in his look, which arose particularly from a tooth which projected forwards, and could only be covered by his lip with effort." Despite the description just quoted, his contemporaries considered him "a fine looking man."

Mason had a criminal tenacity from an early age. Before he turned twenty, he engaged in illegal pursuits. While a teenager, he attempted to steal a horse, and in the chase that followed, the owner shot him. Mason didn't serve any serious jail time for the crime, and after recovery, he moved a short distance from Charles Town. There he did various jobs ranging from tracking down runaway slaves to capturing wild horses.

Mason didn't have any other major run-ins with the law before the Revolutionary War. At the outbreak of the Revolution, Mason joined the Virginia militia and received a commission as Captain. Once his company walked into a Native American ambush near Fort Henry, and most of his men died in the attack. Mason received wounds, but he survived, recovered, and eventually returned to duty. In 1779, Captain Mason took part in a major operation in northeastern Pennsylvania that destroyed ten villages of the pro-British Seneca tribe.

The man who later became America's most notorious river pirate remained in the fight for American independence until at least 1781. Later he served as a Justice of the Peace and, although there is no record that he had legal training, he served as an associate justice of a minor court.

By every indication, Mason was doing well in his virtuous and noble profession, but honest work did not suit him. Perhaps he needed more excitement, or maybe he thought a life of crime would be easier and pay better. Regardless of his reasons, Mason gave up his ethical life and took up piracy.

In the 1790's, Mason relocated his family to the banks of the Ohio River near Henderson, Kentucky. It was about that time that he became a full-time criminal. He founded a gang of pirates that raided flatboats floating the river. The Mason Gang attacked unsuspecting travelers at will, and for a time, they went unchallenged, and he received the title "King of the River Pirates." Mason moved his operation first to Diamond Island, and later, Cave-in-Rock. As noted earlier, the Harpes were part of the Mason's pirate band for a short time before Mason threw them out of the gang.

The number of "exterminators" seeking to drive criminals out of the country continued to pressure him, and Mason decided to abandon his base on the Ohio River and move his operation to safer environs. In March 1800, Mason relocated his family and criminal enterprise to the town of New Madrid in Spanish Louisiana (present-day Missouri).

New Madrid, now the county seat of New Madrid County, Missouri, was the most important village in Spanish upper Louisiana. The frontier settlement was about a decade old, and it consisted of a military post occupied by a small force of soldiers and a town of about 800 citizens. The population was a melting pot of people recently moved there from France, the United States, Canada, or Spain. New Madrid remained under Spanish rule until 1804, when it became part of the United States under the provisions of the Louisiana Purchase.

After relocating, the King of the River Pirates and his gang continued to raid boats, but they also took to robbing travelers along the Natchez Trace. The transition from pirate to highwayman was easy and soon Mason was collecting large sums of stolen gold, horses, and other items from those he robbed and sometimes killed.

Old Natchez Trace began as a Native American trail. After the American Revolution, the road became a major western thoroughfare. It extended approximately 440 miles from Natchez, Mississippi to Nashville, Tennessee. Natchez Trace connected the Cumberland, Tennessee, and Mississippi Rivers, and made trade easier between the west and places including Illinois, Kentucky, and Virginia. A large number of merchants brought their goods down the rivers Ohio and Mississippi on flatboats, sold them, and then returned north with food and other provisions on pack mules and draft horses. Of course, they carried their profits with them too.

The Old Natchez Trace was rife with highwaymen and murders, and strong-armed robberies were commonplace. The Mason Gang was just one of many outlaw combinations terrorizing the Natchez Trace, but it became the most notorious. Mason, like the Harpes, often left his calling card with his murdered victims. Mason was fond of leaving a message after his crimes in the blood of his victims that read: "DONE BY MASON OF THE WOODS." Soon the term "Mason of the Woods" struck fear in the hearts of travelers all along Natchez Trace. Beyond penning messages in blood, Mason also kept the scalps of some of his victims as trophies.

While Mason did not relocate in New Madrid permanently until March 1800, he attacked persons travelling along Natchez Trace and the tributaries it connected years before that. There was so much traffic on the Natchez Trace that Mason and his gang were able to take all the food and clothing they needed to sustain themselves, while taking a considerable amount of coin from their prey. At that time, much of the western Tennessee wilderness was nominally reserved for Native Americans. Mason made most of his raids against American citizens heading north and east through the "Indian nation."

Since the risk of attack was so great, travelers along the Natchez Trace developed a method for protecting their money. They sowed it inside rawhides and hid the hides inside the packs with their supplies. At night, before they made a fire, they removed the hides from the packs and hid them in the bushes a distance from their camps. The idea was that if robbers attacked their camp, their money would be elsewhere. The tactic didn't work well. Those facing death from outlaws usually retrieved their money and handed it over to the thieves without much of a fight. Sometimes handing over their valuables saved their lives, often it didn't.

Wiley Harpe did not suspend his criminal life between the time that his brother died and his falling back in with Mason. After he escaped the McBee posse, Harpe headed south to the Natchez Trace and lived, more or less, among the Choctaws.

Traversing the Natchez Trace several times between Mississippi and Nashville, Tennessee, Harpe took part in several highway robberies. During one trip, the charming Harpe befriended a man named Bass, who lived not far from Nashville in Williamson County, Tennessee. Bass was unhealthy, and Harpe, working a con game, offered him kindness.

Bass was grateful to Harpe, and when they arrived at his father's home, Bass asked Harpe to stay with them for a while. Never one to refuse free room and board, Harpe accepted the offer.

Bass had a sister, and Harpe courted and seduced her. Although Harpe was still married, he wed the bedazzled girl. Then Wiley told the Bass clan that he was taking his new bride to North Carolina to start a new life. The girl's parents evidently consented to their daughter heading east over the Great Smoky Mountains into North Carolina.

East Tennessee was Wiley Harpe's home country, and many of the people there knew him well and could identify him. Since he was a wanted criminal, it is surprising that Harpe would go that way again. When all else fails, fools rely on luck, and apparently Harpe believed his luck would allow him to slip through east Tennessee undetected.

The trip of the newlyweds ended at the north fork of the Holston River in Hawkins County, Tennessee. Harpe came upon a group of slaves working on a farm. He told them his wife's horse had thrown her from her saddle, her feet became tangled in the stirrups, and the horse dragged her to death.

He ordered the slaves to bury his wife, and they did. Then he went into town, sold her saddle and belongings for whatever he could get for them, and rode away mere hours after the "accident" that took his new bride's life.

When the community learned of the woman's death and subsequent burial, some had questions. After some discussion, they agreed to exhume the body. Upon pulling the woman from the grave, their worst fears were confirmed. She did not die from being dragged by a horse. Wiley Harpe had bashed in her head.

Having gotten away with yet another murder, Harpe fled west. After living in Louisiana for a bit, he relocated to Memphis (then called "Chickasaw Bluffs"). Needing a steady income, Harpe enlisted (under the name of John Setton) into the company commanded by Captain Richard Sparks at Fort Pickering. Harpe's ruthlessness served him well, and he quickly earned promotion to the rank of Sergeant. Harpe gained the Captain's complete confidence, and when he told Sparks that he was going on a hunting trip of several days duration, the Captain was more than happy to loan his Sergeant his "elegant rifle." Then Harpe took a canoe filled with provisions and started down the Mississippi. Harpe never returned, and Sparks never saw his beautiful rifle again.

Harpe floated down the Mississippi until he came to the Arkansas River. Steering up that river, he then joined Mason.

The exact date when Samuel Mason allowed Wiley Harpe to rejoin his gang is unknown. It is certain that the outlaw soon rose to the second in command of the organization. After Wiley Harpe rejoined the gang, whether due to his influence or not, they grew evermore violent and murderous.

The continued lawlessness on the Mississippi River and along the Natchez Trace prompted the authorities to action. William Charles Cole Claiborne became the Governor of

Mississippi Territory on May 25, 1801, and within months of taking office, he began efforts to end, or at least slow, the number of robberies and murders in his jurisdiction.

On February 10, 1802, Claiborne directed an official communication to Manuel de Salcedo, the Spanish Governor General of the Province of Louisiana, at New Orleans. Claiborne related to de Salcedo that he had received information about "a daring robbery which had lately been committed upon some citizens of the United States who were descending the River Mississippi on their passage to" Natchez. Claiborne continued that he could not determine if the criminals were Spanish subjects or American citizens.

On February 28, de Salcedo responded to Claiborne with a letter stating, "It is truly impossible to determine whether the delinquents are Spaniards or Americans." The Governor General continued that he had given "the most positive orders to take the most efficacious means of discovering and apprehending the criminal or criminals that can be adopted and I assure your Excellency that if the criminals are taken they will be punished in such a manner as to serve as an example to others."

Despite his promise to punish the criminals, de Salcedo blamed the United States for the situation. He said that Americans from "the States and Western Settlements having the freedom and use of the navigation of the Mississippi" had flooded the territory. The Governor General said a large number of the migrants were "vagabonds who have fled from, or who do not, or can not return to, the United States."

Claiborne and de Salcedo shared a sincere desire to rid their territories of the criminal scourge plaguing them, but they faced a sticky problem in the realm of international affairs. Neither governor had any problem with tracking down and arresting highwaymen and river pirates on his own side of the Mississippi. Yet the Spanish would not allow Americans to enter the Spanish zone in pursuit of outlaws. Neither would the Americans allow Spaniards to enter American territory pursuing criminals.

Mason, Harpe, and the gang understood the situation and used it to their advantage. They cleverly made a point of not committing any crimes in Spanish territory. They reasoned that no matter how notorious they became, no matter how hated, no matter how wanted, they had a permanent safe haven on the Spanish side of the line as long as they confined their crimes to American territory.

Sometimes a single event, or a few closely connected events, can be the impetus for authorities to take drastic action. The robbery of Colonel Joshua Baker led directly to the end of the Mason Gang, and to the death of Samuel Mason and Wiley Harpe.

Colonel Baker was a successful merchant residing in central Kentucky. He made yearly excursions south on flatboats carrying produce and horses to New Orleans. In the spring or summer of 1801, Baker, after selling some of his goods and trading the rest, began his long ride home. Along with Baker on his return trip were four men on good horses. Baker also brought back with him five pack mules loaded down with provisions and other things, including the proceeds he received from his transactions in New Orleans.

Baker and his party met with no trouble until they began to cross a large creek in Hinds County, Mississippi, on August 14, 1801. The creek, about twenty miles from Jackson, was slow to ford, and rendered those crossing it vulnerable to attack. The party, unaware of any danger, watered their horses and mules before making their way across. Then suddenly, Samuel Mason and three of his men surprised Baker's caravan.

The victims had no opportunity to defend themselves, and they could do nothing but surrender "their horses, traveling utensils," and about "twenty-five hundred piasters in gold, silver and banknotes." Yet the loss was not as great as it could have been. The commotion the bandits caused spooked one of the pack mules and it bolted away. The robbers were in a hurry to get away, and didn't have time to collect the frightened animal and take the goods and money it carried.

There are several accounts, not included here, purporting to detail what happened after the gang robbed Baker and his party. These stories, romantic as they are, are all different, and there is nothing factual that proves one is more accurate than the others. They do all agree that Baker never recovered his goods or money stolen in this encounter with the Mason Gang.

The Baker robbery was just one of the many attacks done by highwaymen along the Natchez Trace. It matters to this story only because it led to the end of Wiley Harpe.

Colonel Baker's business required continued use of the Mississippi River and the Natchez Trace. In fact, the loss of his money in August 1801, hastened him to make another trip. In April 1802, he loaded a flatboat with merchandise and started down the Mississippi again. Baker was determined not to lose his goods on this trip. He laid in a large supply of guns, to both protect his boat and for his possible use when he rode up the ever-dangerous Natchez Trace on his way back to Kentucky.

Baker floated down the "Mighty Mississippi" to a point below Vicksburg, then known as Walnut Hills. There, Mason and some of his men attempted to commandeer Baker's flatboat, but Baker and his stoutly armed crew repelled the attack.

Baker believed that only action by some agency of the American government could put an end to Mason and his ilk. The Colonel penned a report of Mason's second raid on his possessions and had it delivered to Governor Claiborne. Upon reading the report, Claiborne realized that his efforts to curb the outlaw infestation in his territory were failing. Prompted to further action, on April 27, Governor Claiborne sent three official letters from his capital at Washington, Mississippi.

The first he had delivered to Colonel Daniel Burnett, commander of the Claiborne County militia at Fort Gibson.

The Governor's letter expressed, with a sense of urgency, the need to stop the river pirates and highwaymen. It began by informing Burnett that a band of robbers "alternately infest the Mississippi River and the road leading from this district to Tennessee, rendezvous at or near the Walnut Hills, in the County of Claiborne."

The Governor identified Samuel Mason and Wiley Harpe by name as the leaders of the banditti that attempted, unsuccessfully, to seize Baker's flatboat. Claiborne continued, "These men must be arrested; the honor of our country, the interest of society, and the feelings of humanity, proclaim that it is time to stop their career. . ." Claiborne reminded the Colonel that Wiley Harpe's crimes "are many and great, and in point of baseness, Mason is nearly as celebrated . . ." He told Burnett that as long as "these sons of rapine and murder are permitted to rove at large, we may expect daily to hear of outrages upon the lives and properties of our fellow citizens."

The Governor realized that Burnett's militia wasn't an organized fighting force, but a group of untrained civilians that came together only when needed. Claiborne requested that Burnett round up "fifteen or twenty men as volunteers" and lead them to Walnut Hills. There, they were to question anyone that might have information about the whereabouts of Mason and Harpe. Then they were to search the woods as far as Yazoo, which was fifty miles to the northeast.

The Governor further ordered that if the militiamen made contact with the Mason Gang, they were to "use all means" in their power "to arrest them, or any of them." The Governor said that if Burnett arrested some or all the Mason Gang, he was to transport them "under a strong guard to Natchez."

The Governor informed Burnett that he had also written Lieutenant Seymour Rennick, commander of a detachment of United States troops at Grindstone Ford on the Natchez Trace. Claiborne stated that Rennick would "provide all the aid in his power" in capturing Mason, Harpe, and their band of outlaws.

Claiborne finished his letter with the enticing promise of a "very generous reward" for "taking these lawless men."

Governor Claiborne's message to Lieutenant Rennick related the attack of Baker's boat, and continued that Samuel Mason and Wiley Harpe (both mentioned by name) "have been in the habit of committing with impunity murders and robberies." The Governor said he thought the two men were probably "at or near the Walnut Hills."

Claiborne had no direct authority over Lieutenant Rennick, and he simply asked that the federal government provide a sergeant and twelve men in support of Colonel Burnett. The governor was confident that Rennick would lend assistance.

Governor Claiborne addressed his third message "To the Officer commanding the United States Troops near the mouth of Bear Creek on the Tennessee River." Again mentioning Harpe and Mason by name, he informed the officer "the road from this territory to Tennessee is infested by a daring set of robbers."

The Governor requested that if the officer "should receive information of any mischief being done or attempted in the wilderness you will immediately order out a party of men, and make the necessary exertions to arrest the offenders."

The lower Mississippi had long since grown accustomed to lawlessness and wanton bloodshed, but the terror now brought to the frontier by Mason was beyond the pale. But Mason was, in the minds of the populace, the second worst monster in Mississippi Territory. Although no one knew for sure where Wiley Harpe was, most assumed he was in Mississippi. Harpe was, by this time, the most infamous outlaw in America. Stories of Harpe's atrocities drifted like a hot breeze throughout the six hundred miles between Natchez and Knoxville. The same wind blew across the six hundred miles from New Orleans to the Illinois border.

As noted earlier, Wiley Harpe escaped the McBee posse and disappeared. For the next two years, while still a wanted outlaw, he managed to avoid attention. Until seen in the company of Samuel Mason in April 1802, no one reported any credible information regarding Wiley

Harpe. There were no bodies found bearing the Harpe signature disposal method of rocks in the chest. Nor were there any murders ascribed directly to the smaller Harpe at all. For a considerable time, the general opinion – hope really – was that Wiley Harpe had fled the United States, or better, someone had killed the murderer. Of course, now that proof positive existed that Harpe was in the lower Mississippi, fear spread across the wilderness like a wildfire.

A theory developed that Governor Claiborne didn't believe that Harpe was one of Mason's men. He, so goes the theory, simply joined the names of Harpe and Mason together to inflame the community and cause the citizens to pursue Samuel Mason more actively. If this was true, it was a mighty consequence that Harpe was indeed the second in command in the Mason Gang.

True to what he told Colonel Burnett, Governor Claiborne "offered a liberal reward for" Mason and Harpe "dead or alive . . ." The reward offered may have grown to as high as $2,000. If so, it included offers by private citizens to augment the reward offered by the government. In 1804, Claiborne wrote Secretary of State James Madison stating, "A reward of four hundred dollars for apprehending them was offered by the Secretary of War [James Dearborn], and five hundred dollars by myself, in my character as Governor of the Territory." The large reward serves as proof of the importance officials put on eliminating the Mason Gang and its leaders. The ploy eventually worked; the $900 reward offered for Mason became the web that trapped Harpe.

The common belief developed that immediately after his brother died, Wiley Harpe sought out Samuel Mason and rejoined his gang. There is no evidence to support that contention. The Harpes barely got out of Cave-in-Rock with their lives, and one would suppose that Wiley would be wary of contacting Mason again. Beyond that, there is no record of Wiley Harpe working with Mason before 1802. It may have been that Harpe joined the Mason Gang and kept a low profile for a while, but no one knows for sure.

On the other hand, Wiley Harpe was the number two man in Mason's Mississippi gang. One would assume that Harpe would have had to work himself up in the organization. Another thing indicating that Harpe was with Mason for a considerable time before April 1802, is the fact that Mason's robberies and murders grew ever more brutal. It is possible that Wiley Harpe influenced Mason to commit ghastly crimes. Regardless of why he did it, the dreadful crimes Mason committed made him, next only to Wiley Harpe, the most wanted man in Mississippi.

The efforts to rid the area of highway robbers and river pirates were somewhat successful, and the authorities arrested several scoundrels. Yet the two most wanted miscreants, Wiley Harpe and Samuel Mason, eluded capture. Harpe succeeded in remaining free mostly because of his legendary luck, but Mason survived by using his brains.

One trick outlaws employed was the tactic of never making camp in the same place for very long. They hid out in any convenient place, but in a few days, they moved on. For a time, the Mason Gang headquartered their operation about twenty miles northeast of Natchez, near present-day Fayette, Mississippi.

Interestingly, many years later, Fayette received a visit from another famous outlaw. In 1879, Jesse James and his gang robbed a store in Fayette of about $2,000.

When the Mason Gang attacked the Baker flatboat, they based their operation near Rocky Springs, a much-used resting place on Natchez Trace, situated about forty miles northeast of Natchez and twenty miles south of Vicksburg. Of course, when the searchers located the hideout, they found that Mason, Harpe, and the other gang members had abandoned the place.

The Mason Gang also spent time in the little town of Palmyra, likewise south of Vicksburg. They also hid out on Stack Island (aka Crow's Nest). Stack Island was near the mouth of Lake Providence, in Spanish Louisiana, and about fifty-five miles south of Vicksburg. When the militia first went after the gang, they learned that the criminals camped at Stack Island. According to one account, "After the Governor's proclamation had been issued Mason and his gang were closely hunted by the whites and Indians and, having made some narrow escapes, they quit the country and crossed the Mississippi to somewhere about Lake Providence in the then Spanish territory."

The situation was ideal for the outlaws. They could commit crimes on the American side of the Mississippi River, then slip across to the Spanish side, and no one could pursue them. This afforded them a free hand to move into the great Spanish wilderness of present-day northern Louisiana and Arkansas. Beyond that, since the gang did not commit crimes in Spanish territory, the Spanish held them in general indifference.

Mason and Harpe knew there was a reward for them "dead or alive." Harpe had been under such a death warrant for a considerable time, but not Mason. Mason discovered Governor Claiborne's proclamation among the effects of a traveler that the gang had robbed. It might have frightened another type of man, or at least caused him retrospection, but not Mason. In fact, he "indulged in much merriment on the occasion."

Mason felt that the proclamation proved the authorities feared him, and the terror that the Governor's statement caused would benefit his gang of conspicuous outlaws. By this time, Mason had grown as arrogant as his partner, Wiley Harpe. He believed he could outmaneuver – and outthink – any detachment of militiamen or any civilian posse that might pursue him. Of course, all he had to do was to make it to Spanish territory to defeat his pursuers.

Far from curtailing their dastardly careers, Mason and Harpe broadened and intensified their attacks. In May 1802, they were attacking flatboats on White River (in present-day

Arkansas), more than 100 miles north of their usual haunts. One such attack drew attention to the Mason Gang, in particular. On a windy May morning, as a flatboat drifted south on the White River, they noticed two long canoes beside which were twelve heavily armed men on the shore.

The men yelled out to those on the slow moving boat and asked them to pull it up to the shore. Those on shore said they wanted to purchase rifles. Cautious, those on the flatboat refused the invitation and continued on their way. The pirates then jumped in the canoes and gave pursuit, but the wind hampered them and they never caught up to their intended prey. There was no doubt that the Mason Gang had initiated the assault on the lucky men on the flatboat.

Not every boat coming down the White River received aid from a strong wind. About two weeks after the incident mentioned above, Mason's Gang "attacked a merchant boat and took possession of her, after having killed one of the people on board."

15. Wiley Harpe Testifies

THE robberies on the Mississippi and the Natchez Trace continued through 1802 and 1803, with increasing frequency. Mason's Gang did not commit all the acts of piracy and highway robbery, but they committed more than their share of them. Mason gained such notoriety from the brutal assaults he oversaw that he became almost as infamous as the reviled Wiley Harpe.

Needing a new hideout, Mason decided he'd return to New Madrid and again make it his base of operation. Of course, he chose New Madrid because Americans desiring justice, or a cut of the $900 price on his head, couldn't get to him. More than 400 miles north of Natchez and in foreign territory, Mason believed he was as safe from his pursuers as if he were camping on the moon.

As a prelude to New Madrid, the Mason Gang made camp about 35 miles south of there near Little Prairie (now Caruthersville, Missouri). On a cold winter morning in January 1803, a detachment of Spanish soldiers suddenly surrounded the hideout. Mason was surprised, but not worried. He didn't believe he had anything to fear from the Spaniards, and he didn't put up a fight. After all, his crimes had all been committed on the American side of the Mississippi. He was confident that the Spaniards would release him quickly.

What Mason didn't know was the amount of external pressure the Spanish felt. Spain had ceded the Louisiana Territory back to France in 1800, but still maintained nominal control of it. Under pressure from the French to crack down on outlaws, the Spanish had taken a more active interest in arresting those who were raiding merchants on the Mississippi and rivers leading into it. More importantly, the American government peppered the Spanish Governor General with complaints about the large number of criminals taking sanctuary in Spanish Louisiana.

Moreover, the Spanish were not certain that Mason had confined his raiding to American territory. If he had committed crimes in Louisiana, the Spanish desired to punish him for it.

Mason told the Spanish soldiers he was a poor, simple farmer, and that his enemies wrongly accused him of the crimes with which he was charged. The problem with Mason's defense was that when they searched him, the soldiers found condemning evidence in his baggage. Most farmers made no more than a few dollars a year, but Mason had the staggering sum of $7,000 on him. When asked about it, Mason offered the lame explanation that he had found the King's Ransom he carried "in a bag hanging on a bush near the road." Evidently, Mason hoped to convince the Spaniards that some traveler had hidden their money and then left without it. The ploy didn't work. The Spaniards found Mason's explanation utterly absurd, and his story about finding the money more suspicious.

Even more damaging to Mason's claim that he was just a poor, honest farmer was the discovery of "twenty twists of human hair of different shades which do not seem to have been cut off voluntarily by those to whom the hair belonged." Of course, the fact that Mason had 20 human scalps, some of which he had undoubtedly taken from white men, was evidence impossible for him to explain away.

The evidence convinced the Spaniards to arrest Mason, his family, and the members of his gang that they found with him. They then transported the whole menagerie to New Madrid for a court hearing to determine if Mason was guilty of being a highwayman and river pirate. The hearing took three days.

On January 19, 1803, the Commandant called one of Mason's men, identifying himself as John Setton, to testify. The man with the flaming red hair was, in fact, Wiley Harpe. Despite the many times Harpe's description circulated in Mississippi and Louisiana, no one in the courtroom ever positively identified this man, calling himself John Setton, as the slimy murderer Wiley Harpe.

[Authors note: The court records dealing with this hearing refer to the crimson-haired witness as "John Setton." But in order to avoid confusion, I refer to him by his real name, Wiley Harpe, throughout.]

Harpe did not intend to die any time soon, and he decided he could most easily escape the noose by accomplishing a few things. He had to convince the court that he was a victim of Mason's, and that he committed crimes against his will. He also had to make sure that no one discovered he was, in fact, the long-hunted and universally hated Wiley Harpe.

Harpe began his testimony by admitting he had changed his name from John Setton to John Taylor. But, according to him, Samuel Mason demanded it. He continued that he believed Mason had a special purpose for insisting that he take the name John Taylor.

Harpe was almost gleeful when he confirmed that he "could give much information regarding robberies" committed by the Mason Gang. Harpe then wove a self-serving story, stitched loosely with lies.

He said he was a native Irishman, and that he didn't come to America until 1797. Harpe continued that he joined the United Sates Army and served for a time in Major Geyon's Corps, but had "deserted near the high coast." After his desertion, he moved south of Vicksburg, where he "worked for three weeks for His Majesty the King of Spain." From there he took the "row galley" *Louisiana* to New Orleans, and that winter he found work as a carpenter.

Harpe continued his story by saying that for about two years, he roamed around the Spanish territory, making his living either working for white people or hunting with members of the Choctaw tribe. Then, while he was in Arkansas, an American officer recognized him as an Army deserter and ordered him delivered to a Spanish post. The Spanish handed him over to the Americans, and the Americans lodged him in jail.

Wiley Harpe, still hiding behind his alias of John Setton, continued that while he was in jail, he met a prisoner named Wiguens. Over the next month, the two men became allies and worked out an escape plan. Then, when the opportunity presented itself, they broke out of jail and hurried away.

The two men returned to Arkansas, where a military commander grew suspicious of them and had them confined for 28 days. Unable to prove the men had committed any crime, the commander ordered them released.

Remaining together after their release, they worked for a month on a farm owned by a man named Gibson. Gibson obtained a permit for them to go hunting on White River. They hunted their way downriver, then crossed over to "Little Prairie of the St. Francis River." There, they sold the skins they had collected to a man named Fulsom.

Harpe told the court that they continued their trip because he "wished to join his family in Pennsylvania." Then, on May 14, 1802, he and Wiguens were at about to cross the Mississippi when they, quite by accident, met John and Thomas Mason, a different man named Gibson, and another man named Wilson. Harpe said he remained with the Mason Gang for the next eight months, and then the Spanish arrested him.

Not knowing the identity of the man he was questioning, the Commandant asked the witness if he knew "the man Harpe", and the outlaw, sure he could keep the truth hidden, answered that he had met a man by that name once. He continued that he met a Harpe in the Cumberland area, but that authorities had killed that man later.

Then Harpe, toying with the court, said that the dead man named Harpe had a brother, but he knew nothing about him. He continued that he did not know if Wiley Harpe and Samuel Mason had ever had dealings or had ever met. He further continued that he was certain that Harpe had not been associated with the Mason Gang since May 1802.

The Spanish officials knew little about the previous activities of the Harpes, or Mason for that matter, and the story this bloody brother spun seemed plausible enough to them. Yet the whole tale up to that point had virtually no truth in it. The court accepted the fact that their witness went variously by the names Setton, Taylor, and Wells. Samuel Mason claimed that he used other aliases as well, but when Mason could not recall them, the Spanish disregarded Mason's contention.

The names Setton, Taylor, and Wells were unknown to the Spaniards, and there was no evidence that anyone going by any of those names had committed any crime. This lack of evidence created in the Spanish authorities the mistaken notion that their star witness might be innocent of any crime. This error very nearly allowed Wiley Harpe to escape justice again.

Samuel Mason certainly knew that the witness calling himself Setton was actually Wiley Harpe, but he could not admit it. Mason could not expose Harpe without putting a noose around his own neck. This left Mason with no choice except to hold his tongue and let the windy witness blow lies to every corner of the courtroom.

Harpe was just getting started. He said that when he met the Mason Gang, John and Thomas Mason took everything he owned. These sons of Samuel Mason then asked him to stay with them. As an inducement, they promised to provide him land onto which he could move his family. They also contracted with him "to go after Mother Mason" with them. Mrs. Mason had sometime earlier abandoned her husband Samuel Mason, and her sons, because of their outlaw ways. Mrs. Mason was "generally respected as an honest and virtuous woman by all her neighbors" and she could not abide the lawlessness of her family.

Harpe told the court that from the day he met them, the Masons held him "like a prisoner." They never provided the property they promised him, and they never initiated their plan to kidnap Mrs. Mason. Yet they never released him, and he never had an opportunity to escape. He said the Masons did let him go armed, but they never allowed him more than two rounds of powder at any one time.

He told the court that the Masons did not command him to steal horses, but they expected him to do so. Further, he implied that he didn't steal any. Harpe did say the Masons brought in and took away a number of horses, but he never asked any questions about where they got them. He told the court he did know that the Masons struck a deal with a man named Burton at Little Prairie, in which Burton would pay them $20 each for every horse they brought him which were valued at $60 or more.

Harpe said the Masons left home sometimes "to repair a chimney," and if they were away for several days, they would say they "could not cross the water," "lost their repairing tools," "were hindered by bad weather," or "visited friends," but they never told him whose chimney they had repaired. He offered no explanation as to why, when the Masons were off repairing chimneys, he didn't just wander away from their home and escape.

Harpe's long, winding testimony continued. He said he and the Masons were at the home of Charles Colin in Vicksburg when an American citizen called Mr. Koiret stopped by unannounced. The friendly visit soon turned violent. The Masons determined that Koiret would be a promising target for robbery. While the Masons were working out their plan, Harpe and Koiret remained outside, chatting. Harpe said he found Koiret "an interesting conversationalist."

As they talked, Koiret remarked that he was merely passing through while searching for outlaws guilty of committing crimes along the Natchez Trace and the Mississippi River.

Realizing that their intended victim was an officer of the law, John Mason asked to speak with Harpe privately. Feeling it too dangerous to attack the lawman, the other Masons endeavored to "speed the parting guest" and tried to give the peace officer the bum's rush.

The witness with the flaming mane said he came around the corner of the house with John Mason at his side, and suddenly Samuel Mason appeared. The pirate drew his dagger and ordered "Silence!" Meanwhile, John Mason grabbed Harpe, and the father and son gagged him, tied his hands, and dragged him into the house. After about three hours, the Masons, certain that Koiret was out of the area, removed the gag and bonds, but they continued to guard their victim until the next day.

Harpe swore that shortly after the Masons loosened his ties, Samuel Mason put a written statement before him. The confession stated that Harpe, using the alias John Taylor, led men named Phillips, Fulsom, Gibson, Wiguens, Bassett, along with unnamed others, in one or more of three robberies. The three offenses included in the statement were the Baker robbery, the Owsley robbery, and the Campbell and Anthony Glass robbery.

Samuel Mason said he and his sons were going to take Harpe to a nearby Justice of the Peace and turn him over for trial. Mason continued that if Harpe didn't make a full confession to the three robberies, the Masons would kill him before he had the opportunity to tell anyone the truth. Of course, the purpose of the confession was to absolve Mason and his sons of any involvement of the crimes.

Harpe told the court that the Masons took him to the home of William Downs, a Justice of the Peace living just south of Vicksburg. Along the way, Harpe noticed that the sons, John and Thomas, were carrying loaded rifles, but their father was unarmed.

When they arrived at the Downs residence, the Mason sons positioned themselves outside the house, prepared to kill their captive if he made a misstep. Samuel Mason went inside with Harpe. Downs was a conscientious public servant. He followed proper legal form and accepted Harpe's false confession to the three robberies.

The first confession dealt with the already related robbery of Colonel Baker on the Natchez Trace. Harpe told the Spanish court he could prove that he took no part in robbing Baker. At the time of the raid, he, according to his word alone, was in jail in Arkansas. He also stated his opinion that part of the $7,000 found on Mason at the time of his arrest was the proceeds from the Baker robbery.

"The second crime," resumed Harpe, "was the one committed on the Mississippi" where the Mason Gang robbed a "store boat" belonging to a man named Owsley.

Merchants floated down the river, peddling goods from store boats to persons waiting on shore. This was a valuable service to those needing goods but who found it difficult to get into town to shop.

The Masons wanted to give the impression that Harpe and Phillips were the culprits in the Owsley robbery. Harpe swore that he didn't take part in the robbery. He further stated that Phillips did nothing more than purchase two guns from Owsley. Harpe said that the Masons purchased the remainder of the guns, and then turned the weapons on Owsley and robbed the boat.

The third robbery that Mason wanted to pin on Harpe, Phillips, and the others was one that took place on "the road from Kentucky to Natchez." There, the Mason Gang robbed two men named Campbell and Anthony Glass, and made off with several horses, saddles, and some money. Someone nailed a sign to a tree near the site of the robbery that read, "DONE BY MASON OF THE WOODS."

The Commandant asked Harpe if he thought Mason was guilty of robbing Campbell and Glass. He said he didn't know for sure, but the robbery fit the way Mason worked his crimes. Harpe also stated his opinion that Anthony Glass, one of the supposed victims, was actually in cahoots with Mason. Harpe said he was certain that Glass was a poor man in Vicksburg before he began to work with the Mason Gang.

The list of crimes Harpe denied committing seemed endless. He said Mason once proposed they capture a store boat, drown the owner, and sell its goods to Glass for half the price they would normally bring. Mason promised that Glass would pay cash for the goods, and would never betray them to the authorities. Still playing the innocent victim, Harpe told the court that he refused to take part in the scheme. He continued that he suspected Mason actually committed the crime during one of his "chimney repairing" trips, and that Glass probably still had some of the booty from the robbery in his possession.

Harpe then countered some of the physical evidence against him. He said he had never possessed the pistol Samuel Mason presented to Justice of the Peace Downs as evidence against him. He said the Masons stole the pistol during the Baker robbery, and that Sheriff William Nicholson was the original owner of the weapon. According to Harpe, one of the Masons had used a knife to scrape the sheriff's initials from the handle of the pistol. Setton told the court that the pistol was among the items the Spanish authorities had found when they arrested Samuel Mason, and he encouraged them to examine it closely.

Harpe then described some of the other items confiscated during Mason's arrest. He said that two of the saddlebags had been tan "and had large tacks fastened at their corners," and Samuel Mason broke off the tacks and dyed the saddlebags black. He also stated that a trunk they had was red before Thomas and John Mason painted it black.

Playing the eternal victim, Harpe said that all the Masons abused him, but that Thomas Mason, at times, "seemed somewhat human." Harpe related that Thomas Mason told him that Samuel Mason "had been a thief and a rascal for more than forty years."

Mason was proud of his prowess as a thief, or at least Harpe said he was. The redheaded witness said that once "after taking three measures" of whiskey (that is, three 1.5 ounce shots of liquor), Mason bragged that he was "one of the boldest soldiers in the Revolutionary War" and that "there was no greater robber and no better capturer of negroes and horses than himself." Another time, a drunken Samuel Mason boasted with pride that he had two partners, one named Barret and the other named Brown. These part-time raiders and murderers shared their ill-gotten gains with him in exchange for advice and gunpowder.

Mason enjoyed relating another theft he planned. He laughed as he told the story of how, when his eldest daughter married Philip Briscoe, Mason arranged for Barret, Brown, and several others to wait outside during the ceremony. Then, while the wedding guests were partaking of the bridal feast, the outlaws made off with as many of the horses as they could take with them.

When the wedding guests discovered their horses missing, Mason appeared, outraged. He volunteered to lead a posse to track down and punish the scoundrels. A few days later, authorities arrested some of those participating in the wedding robbery. The thieves told their captors that Mason had planned the operation. Of course, Mason maintained the claim the thieves made was absurd, and the authorities could not comprehend that anyone could be so stonyhearted as to rob his own guests and then lead a posse after those he hired to commit the crime.

Harpe also made charges against John Mason's wife, Marguerite Douglas. He related that the woman pretended to be sick several times, and requested that her husband call for one Dr. Wales. Harpe contended that she merely wanted "to chat with the physician" and "to force the family cooking upon someone else." Harpe didn't say directly that Marguerite Douglas was a loose woman and that she had a physical relationship with the doctor, but he left that impression.

Harpe also told the court about the violent nature of Marguerite Douglas. He said that once Barret, angry because the Masons had not given them as much of the loot as was promised, threatened to turn the whole family in to the authorities. Upon hearing the threat, Douglas became apoplectic. She rushed at Barret, knocked his hat off his head, and shrieked, "Monster, you are not going to denounce me or any of us!" Then she grabbed a butcher knife and tried to plunge it into Barret's heart, but Thomas Mason restrained her. Thomas said, "It is better to part as friends than to part after a fight," and she calmed down. Barret left the place with his life, but without the money owed him.

While the court took no notice of it, there were rumors that the witness was actually Wiley Harpe. On January 24, a witness gave a written statement, declaring that there was a prisoner "who calls himself Taylor but who is supposed to be that notorious villain and murderer Harpe." The court wasn't interested in pursuing the matter, and Wiley Harpe once again was lucky to escape being exposed.

On January 20, the day after the man the Spanish knew as Setton left the stand, the Commandant called Samuel Mason forward to answer more questions. Mason could not tell the court that Setton was actually Wiley Harpe. To do so would have meant death for all the accused, and he knew it. With no other choice, he went along with the Harpe's ruse, and spun a web of lies equal to Harpe's.

Mason admitted he had detained Harpe, but that he had justification for it. Mason explained that when bandits robbed Owsley's boat in April 1802, rumors flared up that he and his sons had committed the crime. Mason continued that Owsley did not know the identity of those that attacked him and his five boatmen. Yet when describing the incident, he recounted two peculiarities that distinguished the case from any other.

First, after the bandits plundered the boat, one of the three outlaws handed $5 to a crewmember that suffered serious wounds during the brief but intense gun battle. Second, after the hijacking, the pirates hammered a sign to a nearby tree that read, "DONE BY MASON OF THE WOODS."

John and Thomas Mason, according to their father, heard the account of the Owsley robbery several times, and in each case, those relating details of the incidents claimed that Samuel Mason was the ringleader of the attack. Then one day, John and Thomas came upon two strangers. One said his name was "Setton" and the other told the Masons his name was "Wiguens." After riding along with the Masons for a few hours, the one identified as Setton admitted that he, Wiguens, and a man named Gibson were part of the gang that robbed Owsley. This man Setton also admitted he gave the wounded man $5, and then nailed the sign to the tree implicating Samuel Mason.

While the Masons rode along with two of the men that committed the crimes the authorities wanted Samuel Mason for, they decided to convince the two outlaws to throw in with them. Then, when the time was right, they would force the highwaymen to admit their crimes publically and absolve the Mason family of the crime. They succeeded in detaining the man called Setton, but Wiguens got away.

Samuel Mason continued his testimony by relating his defense regarding the assault on Colonel Baker's boat. Mason said a few days after the pillaging of his boat, Baker came to the Mason home near Natchez. When Baker saw him, the outraged victim demanded the arrest of Thomas Mason. Baker said, "I could pick him out of a thousand."

Samuel Mason explained to the Spanish court that Baker was mistaken because John Mason and the man Wiguens looked very much alike. Mason continued that Wiguens had told John Mason in private that he, Harpe, Bassett, Fulsom, Phillips, and others took part in the Baker robbery.

Mason related that (according to Harpe) Bassett, Fulsom and Phillips told Baker they needed the weapons for use in their hunt for the Mason Gang, and they paid cash for all the firearms Baker had on hand. After they left the boatmen unarmed, others of their group appeared and robbed Baker of all his cash and all his goods they could carry.

The man Fulsom, again according to Mason, told his fellow raiders not to be concerned about Baker forming a posse and coming after them. Fulsom promised them that he could rapidly muster and command a band of 500 Choctaws, and annihilate Baker and his pursuit party without difficulty.

Harpe, so alleged Mason, laughed and remarked at the irony of the situation. He commented how strange it was that two men resembling each other as much as Thomas Mason and Wiguens, were both "involved" in the same crime, and the innocent man found himself accused. A short time later, Wiguens got away from the Masons, and from then on, they kept a close guard on Harpe.

Then Samuel Mason talked about the second attempt to rob Baker. He said that Baker and a posse came to arrest John Mason, and that the younger Mason, believing he could easily prove his innocence, surrendered without a fight. Samuel continued that John's exoneration would have been immediate, but Bassett's associates refused to admit they had seen John Mason miles away from the robbery at the very time Harpe and the others were committing it.

After John Mason (according to his father) had spent about two months in jail, "he was liberated by men who did not make themselves known to him." Of all the lies Mason told in court, this was perhaps the least plausible. It is impossible to believe that anyone would risk his life breaking another out of jail and never reveal his name. The first appearance of Zorro was more than a century in the future.

Samuel Mason said that after the jailbreak, John Mason was free, but had no safe place to go. The Baker robbery occurred in American territory and the Owsley robbery in Spanish territory, and John had no safe haven in which to retreat. He hid in the woods for weeks, hoping suspicion would fall on someone else, but it did not. Instead, "suspicion against him and against the entire Mason family grew stronger day by day."

Samuel Mason stipulated to the fact that he took Wiley Harpe before Magistrate William Downs. He explained that he took a number of items from Harpe and held them as evidence to prove the innocence of the Masons. He admitted he still had the items for which the Spanish arrested him in Little Prairie.

Mason continued that he had pleaded with Harpe to tell the truth in front of the Justice of the Peace, and that Harpe "consented to do so." Then, Mason said he and Harpe went "about twelve miles below" Vicksburg, to the office occupied by William Downs. Mason said that, among other things, he had a pistol with him that Harpe took from the Owsley vessel.

Mason told the Spanish court that Downs "received Setton's confession but was not able to take his oath, as he had no sheriff on guard with him." Mason then left the magistrate's home, leaving Harpe there. Mason did not tell Harpe that he intended to locate Anthony Glass. Mason said he believed that Glass held half-interest in the Owsley boat, and could bear witness to the fact that Harpe was guilty of the robbery.

When Mason proposed that Glass return to the Justice of the Peace with him, Mrs. Glass objected. She pleaded with her husband not to testify against Harpe. Her brother, one Bassett, had participated in several robberies, and she feared that if her husband exposed Harpe, authorities would jail her brother.

Glass placated his wife by telling her that Harpe was an army deserter and no one would believe anything he said. Glass continued that after he denounced Harpe, the military would take the deserter into custody, and that would be the end of the affair. Finally, Mrs. Glass relented, and Mason and Glass left for the magistrate's office.

When Mason and Glass arrived, their hopes of having Harpe locked up dissolved. Soon after Mason departed, Harpe "suspecting some trickery, had left." Technically, Harpe was not under arrest, and Downs had no authority to hold him.

Samuel Mason told the Commandant that a few weeks after Harpe had made his escape, he rejoined the Masons and had been with them ever since. Mason had not heard Harpe's testimony, but he told the court, "If Setton told the truth in the testimony he gave in this trial, our statements must agree." Samuel Mason finished his testimony by requesting that the

Spanish authorities refrain from turning him over to the American authorities.

On the morning of January 21, John Mason appeared before the Commandant. Most of his testimony agreed with that of his father's. John Mason told the court that he had been trying for a very long time to "vindicate" and "establish" himself, and to live "a decent life." He related that he had escaped prison because there was no way for him to defend himself while behind bars.

John Mason said that he knew nothing about any of the robberies except what he had heard from Wiley Harpe (aliases John Taylor and Wells) and from Druck Smith (alias Smith Gibson). Mason insisted he had never seen Phillips, Fulsom, and the other Gibson.

The Commandant asked him how the Masons came into possession of the eight horses they had when arrested. Although Commandant had not inquired about the horses when questioning any other witness, John Mason had a response. He accounted for each horse by giving a detailed account of its purchase or trade.

The Commandant then asked John Mason why "he pursued the two Frenchmen in a boat until they had reached a safe harbor." He explained that he and his brother Thomas were on the river and they had Harpe in custody. They surmised that the Frenchmen were involved in some of the raids the authorities suspected the Masons of committing. They followed the men, hoping that they could force them to verify the fact that Harpe was guilty of the crimes attached to the Masons.

John Mason said when they got to Vicksburg, they discovered the men they were following were French officials, and they broke off the pursuit. They didn't bother to inform the Frenchmen why they had trailed them for so long.

John Mason swore that most of the money the Masons possessed at the time of their arrest belonged to Harpe. He continued that Harpe claimed he had "found it in a bag hanging on a bush near the road." Harpe also bragged that that he had more money than he could spend. Mason added that he believed Harpe had stolen the money during a recent robbery.

The court record of John Mason's testimony concluded with an interesting sentence. "And the prisoner being asked by the interpreter whether he had anything further to say or anything to unsay, he answered 'No,' but requested, as his father had done before him, that we do not hand him over to the United States Government, and after his declaration was read to him, he persisted that it was true."

Thomas Mason followed John Mason on the witness stand. He more or less confirmed the testimony of his father. He told the court his occupation was "farming and harvesting" and "bringing down flour and whiskey" in flatboats.

Thomas Mason conceded that he had heard about the Baker and Owsley raids, but he said he knew nothing about them except what Harpe had told him.

Thomas Mason said he accompanied Harpe to the office of Justice of the Peace William Downs. However, he denied that he had forced Harpe to present the affidavit to the magistrate. He said that the "Governor of Natchez" had sent a message to John Mason stating that if he could locate a witness willing to confess, it would "tend to clear him of his guilt." That is why the Masons were so interested to have Harpe confess before Downs.

The Commandant then asked Thomas about his activities at Cave-in-Rock, specifically if he recalled a man named Mosique and the two Duff brothers, while in Illinois. He answered that he had heard of them, and he thought that Indians had killed one of the Duff brothers.

To other questions, Mason answered that he knew nothing about robbing a free black man in St. Louis, or a man named Lecompte. He denied any knowledge of stealing a female slave and selling her to a priest named Manuel, as well. When asked if he knew that the Masons stood accused of those crimes, "the witness continued to profess he had never heard of them."

The next witness was Marguerite Douglas, the wife of John Mason. She said she had been married to John for eight years and she had "keen regret" that her husband and the other Masons were "so falsely accused" of various crimes. She said that she knew nothing of the crimes except from hearsay and gossip. She confided to the court that Wiley Harpe told her that commandeering Baker's boat was as easy "as robbing some old woman."

Douglas told the Commandant she knew nothing about the items found with the Masons. She said the money and stolen goods found among her personal belongings did not belong to her. She explained that when packing, she must have been in such a hurry that she placed some of Harpe's personal property into her bag.

Samuel Mason, Jr., testified next. He said he was eighteen, and that he had lived with his parents until he moved out about three months before his arrest. He said his father and brothers had left his mother at Bayou Pierre - between Natchez and Vicksburg – while they went about the process of establishing a new home. He said his mother was now sick and living with her daughter and son-in-law.

The Commandant found Mason's testimony unsatisfactory. The Spaniard chastised Mason, "You ought to speak the truth for you have a mother, who, it is reported, is a good and honorable woman, and you ought not to be mixed up in the wickedness of your father and brothers, who, it is said, are guilty of many thefts and robberies." The young man's responses to the remaining few questions posed to him mirrored those given by his father and brothers.

On January 24, Magnus Mason, the last of the Mason family, testified. He gave his age as sixteen, and said he was born "in Kentucky on the south side of Green River." This is interesting, because all of Samuel Mason's other children testified they were born in the state of Pennsylvania. Magnus Mason testified that he had resided "part of his time with his father in Kentucky and part with his mother in Bayou Pierre near Natchez."

Magnus declared that his father had spent virtually all of the past two years away, endeavoring "to discover men who were committing the robberies" that the authorities blamed on the Masons. This contradicted the testimony of his father, his brother, and Harpe. Yet no one associated with the trial seemed to notice the discrepancy.

Dr. Richard Jones Waters testified next. Waters knew Samuel Mason fairly well, and had recommended the granting of a passport to the man. Waters said he met Mason in either 1791 or 1792, at "Red Banks on the Ohio" (now Henderson, Kentucky). At this time, Waters was already living in New Madrid, but he had been traveling in the east and was on his way home. When he came to the Ohio River, he offered to hire a merchant named Charles Lafond and two others to take him to New Madrid. The three men were on their way to New Orleans, and they agreed to the offer.

When the boat arrived at the Falls of the Ohio (present-day Louisville), Waters told Lafond that he was going to remain there for a few days. Lafond said he would go on to Red Banks, where he intended to sell some of his goods. Lafond promised to await Waters until the doctor arrived at Red Banks.

When Dr. Waters came to Red Banks, he met Samuel Mason for the first time. Mason told Waters that Lafond had gone fishing a few days before, and then had continued south.

Waters never learned if Lafond ever made it to New Orleans. Much later, after learning about the infamy of Samuel Mason, Waters began to wonder if Lafond and his party had met with foul play at the hands of the pirate.

About a year after Lafond stranded him, Waters was again traveling down the Ohio River, and he stopped at Red Banks. He was surprised to meet Samuel Mason again. Mason asked the doctor to come to his house and treat his ailing wife. Waters agreed, and when he arrived, he found Mrs. Mason sick and in bed. Waters treated the woman, and Samuel Mason purchased $70 worth of medicine and goods from him. As was common for frontier folk in those days, Mason had no cash. The doctor agreed to accept $40 worth of fresh meat and a demand note for $30 payable by Felic Concer of New Madrid. When the doctor arrived in New Madrid, he discovered that Concer had moved away, and no one knew where he had gone. In 1798, however, Waters met Mason again, and Mason paid the debt.

The doctor and the pirate met once again in March of 1800. Thomas Mason and a man called Smith were with the pirate. They said they came to New Madrid to get medicine for John Mason's wife, Marguerite. The men offered to trade goods that they claimed they purchased from a store boat for the drugs Marguerite needed, and the unsuspecting doctor agreed.

A few days after trading for the medicine, Samuel Mason appeared at the home of Dr. Waters again. Mason said he needed the doctor's help in procuring a passport for land in Spanish territory. Waters balked at giving the recommendation. While he wasn't certain that Mason was an outlaw, he had doubts about the man's character.

Mason pleaded with the doctor, admitting that unjust rumors had tarnished his family's reputation, and he said that if the good doctor would vouch for him, he would never regret it. Still uncertain, but willing to take a chance, Waters went before the clerk and secured a passport for Mason. At the time of getting the passport, Waters related every fact he knew about the Masons, but he didn't mention any of the scurrilous rumors to which Mason alluded.

The doctor continued that a few days after securing the passport, Thomas Mason told him that he could not settle on the land grant immediately because he had pressing business in Kentucky. Waters gave "some valuable papers for delivery at the Falls of the Ohio." Thomas delivered the papers, but much later than he promised he would. The doctor never asked for an explanation, and Thomas Mason never offered one.

On January 26, the Spanish officials re-examined and inventoried the items they had confiscated from the Masons when they arrested them. They also endeavored to place a monetary value on those items. The Spaniards listed the pistols Harpe testified that Samuel Mason possessed, but that Mason said belonged to Harpe. They also noted the 20 scalps kept as trophies by Samuel Mason.

The inspectors catalogued goods worth about $600, and about $7,000 in silver coins and paper money. However, the inspectors found that much of the paper currency in Samuel Mason's possession "appears to be counterfeit." The Spanish didn't know it, but Mason evidently got the counterfeit money from Peter Alston. Alston will appear later in this narrative.

On January 27, a resident of New Madrid named Francois Derousser came forward and asked to testify. He said he was a native of Illinois, and that in 1791, while he and his family were working their way down the Ohio River, they made a landing near Red Banks. Derousser said that Samuel Mason, who was a stranger to him, stepped up suddenly, shoved a pistol against his stomach, and threatened to kill him if he did not come with the pirate.

Mason led Derousser to a hut, inside which several people sat. When Derousser and Mason entered, Mason shouted to the others, "This is the man who stole my horses and slaves and sold them to the Indians." Then Mason began looking around the hut for a rope with which he could hang Derousser at once. Derousser pleaded with Mason for his life. The poor man told Mason that it would have been impossible for him to steal from Mason. Finally, Mason agreed to postpone the hanging until the next day.

Mason kept Derousser in chains all night, but instead of hanging his captive, he released him. Derousser had no interest in pressing charges. He simply wanted, according to his testimony, to make a few necessary repairs to his boat and then be back on his way.

Derousser told the court that before he departed, Samuel Mason came to him again. This time, Mason had a business proposition for his former prisoner. Mason convinced Derousser to work two months with the Mason boys. Mason promised to give Derousser a large quantity of linen, calico, and bed covers in exchange for his services. Derousser said he needed the items badly, and he accepted the offer.

Derousser told the court that after he had worked for the Masons for the specified two months, they gave him the items just as they had promised. Then, about three hours later, as he made his way to his vessel, Mason and a man called Captain Bradley waylaid him and took back all the goods. That evening, Eustache Peltier helped Derousser get back to his boat and break it out of the ice surrounding it. Finally, after a trip that included bitter cold and hunger, Derousser and his family made it home to New Madrid.

Next, Eustache Peltier testified before the Commandant. Peltier confirmed the statement given by Derousser. Moreover, Peltier added information about Lafond. Peltier said Lafond, a "European merchant with an emporium of goods in New Orleans," had stopped at Mason's house near Red Banks one night about the time Derousser escaped. No one ever saw Lafond or his boat again.

The last witness to testify before the weary Commandant was Pierre Billeth. Billeth was also a resident of New Madrid. Billeth told the Commandant that during a trip on the Cumberland River in 1798, he heard a slave woman tell Rees Jones and James Downs that her master, Samuel Mason, had forced her to dispose of the corpse of one of his victims. She, with great passion and remorse, declared that after Mason robbed and stabbed his victim, he dragged the body to the Ohio River, where he and she threw it into the water.

According to Billeth, Mason had stolen the slave woman, but had lost her somehow. Sheriff James Downs of Kaskaskia Island sold her at public auction to Father Manuel, a priest living near St. Genevieve, Missouri.

Although it was clear that the Masons and Harpe (in the guise of Setton) were thieves, there was no hard evidence that any of the crimes took place on the Spanish side of the Mississippi. There was ample evidence of criminal activity taking place on the American side, however. Regardless of what they thought of the accused, Spanish authorities had no power to punish violations of American law. The New Madrid court chose to send the group of criminals to New Orleans and have them brought before the court there to determine if Mason and his gang had broken Spanish law.

The trial in New Orleans stood to be important because, even if they could couldn't find violations of Spanish law, Governor General de Salcedo had the power, indeed the duty, under an agreement with the United States, to deliver the criminals to American authorities for prosecution.

The preliminary trial of Samuel Mason ended on January 31, 1803. The Commandant ordered a copy of the trial transcript, the physical evidence, and the $7,000 delivered to militia Captain Don Robert McCoy. McCoy received the mission of delivering the items, as well as the prisoners, to the Governor General in New Orleans. There, they would be tried formally "if it so please the Honorable Governor General." Upon receiving the order, McCoy began preparations to float Mason and the other prisoners to New Orleans for trial before the higher court.

16. Another Escape

THE trip down the Mississippi from New Madrid to New Orleans was several hundred miles long, and required more than two weeks to complete. New Orleans was the jewel of Spanish Louisiana, and due to its situation in relation to the Mississippi River and the Gulf of Mexico, it was, as it had been for the past 75 years, the most important city in the region.

In early February 1803, Captain McCoy and his detachment of guards began the trip with their prisoners. McCoy took the most convenient means of conveyance, a flatboat. The crowded flatboat was not very comfortable. Besides the provisions McCoy carried for the trip, he also had the evidence for use at the trial. There were about 17 people aboard. These included Captain McCoy, the interpreter, five men who constituted the guard and crew, seven prisoners, and three children.

Wiley Harpe (still known by his captors as John Setton) was the most tightly guarded person on the flatboat. Any hope of convicting the Masons rested on Harpe turning state's evidence and seeking clemency in exchange for his testimony. He also held the key to exposing other pirates and highwaymen. In fact, if he gave up everything he knew without revealing his own identity, he could have gone a long way towards ending the rampant crime on and around the Mississippi River.

That is not to say that Harpe received any special treatment from McCoy and his men. In fact, the opposite was true. McCoy made sure that Harpe remained chained while aboard, and that someone was always with him. McCoy's reasoning was sound. He feared that Harpe would try to escape on his own, or worse, that Mason – who was also in irons, but had some freedom of movement – would persuade Harpe to help him overcome the crew, and escape. There was also the possibility that Mason would persuade Harpe to devise a new confession that would throw all blame from the shoulders of the Masons.

McCoy and his men thought the Masons were murderers and thieves that deserved hanging, but they believed Harpe was a much lower form of creature than the Masons. McCoy and his men held Harpe in less regard than they would a mangy, chicken-killing dog. Oddly, McCoy and his men formed their opinion without any real knowledge of just how evil Wiley Harpe was.

McCoy found Harpe not just unattractive, but outright repulsive. His countenance was always downcast and fierce, and he had "a suspicious exterior." He was too evil to smile, and McCoy felt the only benefit of keeping this vermin alive was that he might help get Samuel Mason to the gallows.

McCoy and his men saw this crimson-haired bandit as both a murderer fit for a punishment worse than hanging, and an utter fool. If Harpe was guilty of even half the offenses Samuel Mason accused him of committing, there was no legal method of execution harsh enough to exact justice for his crimes.

McCoy thought Harpe proved himself a fool by allowing Samuel to goad him to confess to various nefarious acts. However, as had happened so often before, McCoy and his men underestimated the fiery-haired monster. Despite his maltreatment aboard the vessel and the fact that his neck was close to being in a noose, as close as Mason's was, Harpe felt encouraged. He knew that he held all the cards in this life-and-death poker game. The only person that knew he was Wiley Harpe could not tell anyone. And the authorities, whether they despised him or not, had to, at some point, cut him a deal in order to finally rid their community of Samuel Mason and the scores of others that Harpe could expose.

When Captain McCoy finally arrived in New Orleans, he delivered his prisoners, the evidence, and the court record from New Madrid to the Governor General of Louisiana and his Secretary of War. However, Governor General Manuel de Salcedo and Secretary of War Vidal chose not to hold a trial of their own. After reviewing the transcript from New Madrid, the men determined that while vile crimes were certainly committed, there was no conclusive evidence that any of them took place within Spanish territory.

On March 3, 1803, Governor General de Salcedo forwarded an official communication to the Mississippi Territorial Governor Claiborne. The letter recounted the facts of the case briefly, and stated that the case fell under American jurisdiction.

Claiborne responded with a request that de Salcedo deliver the prisoners to American authorities at Natchez. The Governor General acceded to the request and, in due time, ordered the accused handed over to the Americans.

In late March, Captain McCoy and his men reloaded the prisoners and some of the stolen property found with them, departed from New Orleans, and made their way towards Natchez. A broken mast forced McCoy to stop at Pointe Coupee (almost halfway between New Orleans and Natchez) on March 26, 1803, and try to repair it. "A part of the men were sent on shore to make a new one, and the rest were left to guard the prisoners."

Shortly after some of McCoy's crew left the boat, Mason and his sons somehow "threw off their chains," grabbed a number of guns, and opened fire upon the remaining guards. "Captain McCoy hearing the alarm ran out of the cabin," but before he could take action, Samuel Mason shot him through the chest and shoulder.

Severely, but not mortally, wounded, McCoy got off a shot from his weapon. The ball struck Samuel Mason in the head just above one eye. The blast knocked the pirate to the deck, but he remained conscious. Mason "rose, fell and rose again" and then continued to lead the battle. As the firefight went on, one of the Spanish guards absorbed a gunshot that shattered his arm.

The short and gory engagement soon turned in favor of the Masons. They drove the remainder of the crew off the boat and took control of the crippled vessel.

After nightfall, Mason realized that the Spanish were collecting a force too powerful to withstand. He and his cohorts, including the women and children, departed the boat and got away.

The Spanish began a pursuit of the band of pirates, and even put up a $1,000 reward for Mason "dead or alive." Yet, the slippery eel managed to slither away to safety.

There is no official record proving that Wiley Harpe escaped with the Masons, but he may have. One would think that had Mason and Harpe truly hated one another, Mason would have killed Harpe before disembarking from McCoy's boat. If Harpe didn't abandon the vessel with Samuel Mason, the Spaniards released him. He certainly did not stand trial in Natchez based on the hearing at New Madrid. Regardless of how he came to be free, Wiley Harpe was on the run once more.

17. The End of Wiley Harpe

SAMUEL Mason's plan was to continue to commit crimes on the American side of the Mississippi and recede to the safety of the Spanish side. This plan was shattered when the French retook possession of Spanish Louisiana as a prelude to concluding the deal to sell the entire territory to the United States. The French had no problem with Americans pursuing outlaws on the west side of the Mississippi, and this left Mason without a safe haven.

Now, facing equal danger of arrest on both sides of the line, Samuel Mason spent most of his time in American territory, and continued his criminal enterprise from there. A secondhand account stated, "The Masons have removed to Mississippi where they have of late committed many robberies, but no murders that I have heard of."

On May 31, 1803, witnesses spotted Mason and several others about fifteen miles northeast of Natchez on Choctaw Trace near Cole's Creek. All those in Mason's party were heavily armed. Upon receiving the report that Mason's Gang was once again in the area, the Governor dispatched two detachments of the Jefferson County militia to pursue the King of the River Pirates. The pursuit failed, and eventually the militiamen returned to other duties.

About two months after witnesses saw Mason near Cole's Creek, a man calling himself James May came to a place about twenty-five miles northeast of Natchez, at the now extinct town of Greenville (also known as Hunston and Huntley), Mississippi. The man, pretending to be May, said the purpose of his visit was to inform the authorities of a recent encounter he had with Samuel Mason.

James May was, in fact, Peter Alston. Alston was a horse thief, counterfeiter, river pirate, and highwayman. Alston was likely one of those arrested with Samuel Mason at Little Prairie, who escaped from McCoy's boat with him. However, this is not certain because Alston did not testify at the court hearing.

There is no doubt that Alston was part of the Mason Gang. In fact, he apparently provided the river pirate with counterfeit silver coins.

Alston was one of the many criminals that abandoned Henderson County, Kentucky, because of pressure from the crusading Captain Young and his extermination squad. From Henderson County, May went to Cave-in-Rock and threw in with Samuel Mason's band of pirates. He then followed Mason southwest, and they "worked" the Mississippi River and the Natchez Trace together. But the authorities in Greenville didn't know any of that.

Alston (using his usual alias: James May) went before a Justice of the Peace on July 25 or 26, 1803, and presented the magistrate "sundry articles of property and money." Alston swore he had taken the items "from the notorious

Samuel Mason." Alston continued that he had shot Mason "in the head just above the eye."

Alston testified before the magistrate that when they first met, Samuel Mason had robbed him and taken him prisoner. Then Mason forced Alston to go with him down the Mississippi, where they joined with other Mason Gang members. A few days after being in the company of the gang, they heard gunfire nearby. Mason ordered his other gang members to hide the horses, and he told Alston to hide a skiff. Although Alston said he was a prisoner, Mason apparently had no problem with him going armed. Alston said he took his gun with him when he left to hide the small boat.

When Alston returned from his task, he saw Samuel Mason counting money. Evidently, Mason intended to give each gang member a share before the band dispersed. Mason wasn't paying any attention to him, and the others were still hiding the horses. This set of circumstances afforded Alston an opportunity. He raised his gun, shot Mason in the head, gathered up the loot, put it aboard the skiff, and made his way to Greenville.

The Justice of the Peace evidently didn't think very much of Alston's testimony, because he took no action in the case. A disappointed Alston departed Greenville without a resolution to his claims. It is likely that Alston left the town with the idea that the only reward he could get for Samuel Mason was to bring the pirate in either dead or alive.

It is possible, though unlikely, that Alston was telling the truth about Mason kidnapping him. The story is reminiscent of the story Wiley Harpe's alter ego, John Setton, told. This could prove that Mason made a habit of kidnapping and enslaving people he came across in the woods or on the river. It could also indicate that Alston borrowed Harpe's story and made it his own. There is not enough information available to say for sure, but there is no question that Alston's account lacked credibility.

If Alston was "robbed and taken" by Mason, the aggrieved man might have had revenge on his mind when he went after Mason. Whether he wanted to get back at Mason or not, Alston certainly wanted the reward Mason had on his head.

Alston (still known as James May) and Wiley Harpe (still known as John Setton) met up sometime after Alston left Greenville. They went around together for some time, committing various crimes. One of their offenses was against Elisha Winters. Winters and his party were headed in the direction of New Orleans when the outlaws fell upon them near Bayou Pierre.

Eventually, the two outlaws tarried at Natchez. While there, someone spotted Harpe and recognized him as one of Mason's men. Upon inspection, the authorities found several items taken during the Winters' robbery. Harpe denied any wrongdoing. He said he was in Natchez to turn state's evidence on the Mason Gang, and that is why he had the stolen merchandise. In late October 1803, unconvinced by Harpe's explanation, the Sheriff locked both Alston and him in jail.

Harpe continued to declare his innocence, and he told his jailers that if they would let him lead a posse, he could take them to a place where he had hidden evidence and money that would prove his innocence and Mason's guilt. He assured his captors that the hiding place was not more than two days away by horseback. The proposal intrigued authorities in Natchez, and they sent the Governor a request to allow them to send the posse, headed by Harpe, on the quest.

The arrest of Alston and Harpe, and the stories they told, added fuel to the fire of enthusiasm surrounding those searching for Mason. Not only were the militia units at Natchez and Fort Gibson on alert, but many of the residents of the area were on the lookout for the pirate and his gang of cutthroats. The woods teemed with soldiers and civilians seeking to harvest the tempting reward offered for capturing or killing Samuel Mason. Under those conditions, even one as adroit at avoiding arrest as Samuel Mason was, could not remain free for very long.

The Governor acquiesced to the request to allow Harpe and Alston to form a pursuing party, and their jailers released them for that purpose. However, Harpe and Alston didn't take any volunteers with them when they left the town. The two rode away alone.

Stories abound as to what happened next. However, all of the stories agree that Harpe and Alston caught up with Samuel Mason. One story places the rendezvous at Rodney, Jefferson County, Mississippi, and another puts it a few miles south of there at Lake Concordia, Louisiana. Regardless of the exact location, Harpe and Alston entered Mason's camp without incident.

Upon seeing the pirate, Harpe and Alston told him that they had returned to rejoin his band of outlaws, and Mason accepted the two back without hesitation. This indicates that the discord between Mason and the men was more of an act for the benefit of the authorities than it was true hostility. It also provides solid proof that Alston never shot Mason, making a daring escape from him. Captain McCoy actually fired the round that struck Mason above the eye.

Harpe and Alston had planned from the beginning to cash in on their erstwhile leader's predicament. Yet, they did not dare try to return Mason to the clutches of justice alive. For one thing, they feared that he would gain the upper hand and kill them. Beyond that, they knew Mason could identity them, and if he did, they would swing alongside him on the gallows. The two men, already guilty of several murders apiece, conspired to kill Mason and collect the bounty on his carcass.

The conspirators bided their time, and when Mason was distracted counting plunder, Wiley Harpe came up behind him silently, and with the efficiency of an expert, swiftly rose and brought down a tomahawk, burying the blade in Mason's brain. Feeling the entire body would be too cumbersome to carry back to civilization, Harpe and Alston chopped off Mason's head and left the rest of the corpse for the flies.

Harpe and Alston "in triumph" prepared their valuable trophy and then "took Mason's head to Natchez in the bow of a canoe, rolled up in blue clay, or mud, to prevent putrefaction." Once they arrived at Natchez, they showed it off. "Mason's head was recognized by many, and identified by all who read the proclamation, as the head entirely corresponded with the description given of certain scars and peculiar marks."

Not everyone agreed that head was Samuel Mason's. Governor Claiborne, desiring positive identification, sent his carriage for Mason's wife, along with the order for her to come and identify the head as belonging to the outlaw. When she saw the head, she "positively denied" it belonged to her husband. Yet the evidence was so strong that Mississippi authorities ignored her statement and certified that the head was Mason's.

The pirate's slayers were not able to get their $1,000 bounty and leave immediately because a delay "occurred in paying over the reward, owing to the slender state of the treasury." It is ironic that if the Mississippi territorial government had been able to cover the reward offered for Mason right away, one of the bloody brothers would have escaped justice.

Word that Mason's head was on display drew the morbidly curious from many miles away, hoping to "view the grim and ghastly head of the robber chief." Beyond that, a good number wanted to speak with the men that had brought in the head of the scourge. All indications are that Harpe and Alston enjoyed their newly gained celebrity status, and they didn't give any thought that someone might reveal their real identities.

As much as they liked the hero treatment lavished on them, Harpe and Alston desired to collect their money and be on their way. But something about the two did not seem to fit. Alston had said he was a victim of Mason, and that he had wounded the pirate, yet his story was that Mason had welcomed him back into the gang. As for Harpe, he had testified against Mason, wanting to turn state's evidence against the outlaw, and previously admitted to being a prisoner of Mason, and a member of the Mason Gang. As strange as the situation was, the authorities appeared prepared to accept the stories of May and Setton, pay them off, and send them on their way.

After proving to the state's satisfaction that the head belonged to Samuel Mason, Harpe and Alston went before a judge and attempted to get him to write an order to the governor to pay the reward. "But just as the judge was in the act of making out a certificate, a traveler stepped into the courtroom and requested to have the two men arrested."

This traveler told the judge that he had been inside the local tavern, and then he went into the stable to make sure his horse was receiving proper attention. He saw two horses, each with a peculiar blaze on its face. The man recognized the horses as belonging to two criminals that had robbed him and killed one of his companions on the Natchez Trace. When the man went into the courthouse to make a report, he recognized Harpe and Alston as the two robbers.

The declaration caused a stir. If true, then Alston was no victim, but a murderous cutthroat himself, and Harpe wasn't a fit witness against Mason, but a notorious murderer in his own right. Uncertain about what to do with the two men, the authorities had them confined until they got some answers. Who were the two men that townsfolk had thought were heroes, and had wined and dined for several days? Where did they come from? How did they earn their daily bread?

They knew nothing whatsoever about Alston – not even his real name. They knew Harpe said Mason had treated him badly, and they knew Harpe admitted to traveling under assumed names. Of course, they still didn't know he was, in truth, Wiley Harpe.

Oddly, the Louisiana Purchase was a factor in bringing down Wiley Harpe. In the winter of 1803, Captain Frederick Stump, commanding a company of troops, came to Natchez to help in the transfer of Louisiana to the United States. He established his headquarters there.

When Harpe and Alston came, demanding the $1,000 for Mason's head, Captain Stump saw them and because the "description of Little Harpe so well corresponded with Setton's appearance" Captain Stump "said he believed that Setton was really Little Harpe."

Captain Stump and Governor Claiborne were old friends, and the Captain's word carried weight with the governor. The order went out to all boatmen docking at Natchez, especially those from Kentucky, to see if they could identify Wiley Harpe. Those that said they could came to the jail and looked at the man calling himself John Setton. Five travelers identified the prisoner as Wiley Harpe. Some of the Kentuckians knew Harpe very well. In fact, some had testified in the Harpe case, before Micajah and Wiley Harpe busted out of the Danville jail.

One of them said, before he ever viewed the jailed villain, "If he is Harpe he has a mole on his neck and two toes grown together on one foot." Upon examination, the man calling himself Setton did have a mole in the exact spot where the man from Kentucky said it would be. Added to that, he did have the fused toes just as described.

If the testimony of the Kentuckians was not enough evidence to prove Setton was actually Wiley Harpe, additional evidence came. John Bowman of Knoxville requested to see if he could identify the two prisoners. When he viewed the one with red hair, he immediately told the jailers that it was Wiley Harpe. Harpe said Bowman was wrong, but the Tennessean persisted that his identification was accurate. Bowman finally said, "If you are Harpe you have a scar under your left nipple where I cut you in a difficulty we had at Knoxville." With that, Bowman tore open Harpe's shirt and revealed the scar.

The game was up for Wiley Harpe. His luck, as notorious as he was, had finally abandoned him. Now even if he did wiggle out of his association with the Mason Gang, he could not avoid punishment for the crimes he committed in Tennessee, Kentucky, and at Cave-in-Rock.

Although it was clear that Harpe could no longer hide behind his alias, he continued to persist that he was a victim of mistaken identity. There is no doubt, however, that he knew he would not survive a trial, and he was already thinking of ways to get out of his predicament. It is likely that he was confident he would survive again. He had been in tight situations before, and had always managed to effect narrow escapes.

No one knew yet that James May was, in reality, Peter Alston. In fact, they knew very little about him except that he stood accused of robbery and murder, and that he had proven himself a man of treacherous and cowardly character in the way he deceived and killed Samuel Mason. If his recent dealings were not enough, he knew that it was only a matter of time before Mississippi authorities discovered that he had evaded capture in Henderson County, Kentucky. Of course, when they discovered that, they would soon learn he had also committed murders and robberies with the Mason Gang while at Cave-in-Rock. Alston, like Harp, certain he could expect no mercy, knew that escape was his only hope.

Wiley Harpe and James Alston likely despised each other. Although they had taken part in numerous crimes together, they never became friends. It is likely that each blamed the other for their legal difficulties. There is no doubt that, had the opportunity for a double-cross presented itself, either man would have taken it. Along with their mutual loathing, Harpe and Alston feared each other, and one would have killed the other if it gained him any advantage. Yet under guard and facing certain death, the two utterly deplorable men needed each other.

How Harpe and Alston escaped is uncertain, but they managed it. They fled Natchez, but had no safe place to go. Word of their breakout caused pursuers to canvass the area like a swarm of bees looking for a field of young clover. The outlaws made it only as far as Jefferson County, Mississippi, before searchers overtook them and confined them in jail at Greenville. One of those taking credit for corralling Harpe and Alston was Seth Caston. Later, he "exhibited demands for one hundred dollars for apprehending and bringing to justice" the two outlaws.

In early January 1804, the two desperados went on trial in the Circuit Court in Greenville. Judges Peter B. Bruin, David Ker, and Thomas Rodney presided over the case. The three judges were among the best-known jurists in Mississippi. A year later, Bruin and Rodney presided over former Vice President Aaron Burr's treason trial in Mississippi. Ker would have taken part in that proceeding too, but he contracted pneumonia during the trial of Harpe and Alston, and died soon thereafter.

The grand jury heard the evidence against Harpe and Alston. With little deliberation, its foreman, William Downs, surprised no one when he announced "an indictment of robbery" against each of the two men. Interestingly, Harpe's indictment continued to refer to him as John Setton, even though everyone involved knew by this time that he was Wiley Harpe. Alston's real identity remained unknown, and his indictment read "The Territory against James May." More interesting still is the fact that even though Wiley Harpe was one of the most odious and repugnant killers to ever roam the earth, he did not face a murder rap in this case. Whether the charge was murder or highway robbery didn't matter much, in any important sense. Both carried the death penalty.

The community felt the two repellant prisoners deserved immediate punishment, in the cruelest manner possible. In fact, they would accept nothing less than the hanging of the criminals. Despite this, the territory of Mississippi did not empanel a kangaroo court or a drumhead tribunal to render judgment against them. The territory provided the two men with the fairest trial possible.

First, Mississippi allowed Alston and Harpe separate trials, with Alston's coming first. This favored Harpe because if Alston won acquittal, then it was unlikely that a second jury would convict Harpe. If a jury convicted Alston, then Harpe still had a chance for his day in court.

Mississippi's twenty-four year old Attorney General George Poindexter served as the prosecutor in both trials. Although he was a notorious drinker and gambler, and very young, Poindexter was an able attorney. Later, he served in Congress and was Mississippi's second Governor.

Mississippi provided Alston and Harpe with quality representation too. Their attorneys, men named Breazeale and Parrott, worked hard for their acquittal, or failing that, to have the judges order a mistrial. With the physical evidence stacked against them, the defense attorneys attempted to prevail on technical grounds.

After entering a plea of "Not Guilty", the defense sparred with the prosecution on several points. First, Breazeale and Parrott attempted to have the indictments quashed. They filed "a plea of former acquittal." That is, they claimed the indictment amounted to double jeopardy. The court rejected the argument, rendering the decision that "the plea of former acquittal is not sufficient in law to be considered a sufficient bar to this indictment."

Then the defense claimed the court did not have jurisdiction. They held that the evidence indicated that the alleged "robberies by Mason's men," if they took place at all, occurred in Illinois, Kentucky, Tennessee, Arkansas, Louisiana, or other locales, but there was no hard evidence that any of them happened in Mississippi. The court rejected that argument as well.

Finally, their attorneys presented a writ of *habeas corpus* for Alston and Harpe. The court rejected the writ as well.

The various defense motions were innovative, even ingenious, but they carried little weight with the law. After the court rejected them, there was nothing left to do but try for the impossible: convince the jury that the evidence did not prove the defendants were guilty.

The court record provides scant information about the trial itself, but it indicates that Elisha Winters testified. Of course, the testimony would have been more than enough to convict the two accused men. When the court declined to free Alston and Harpe on technical grounds, the outcome was a forgone conclusion. One jury found Alston guilty, and another convicted Harpe.

On February 4, 1804, the court passed sentence on the two men. Except for the names of the convicted, the sentences were identical. Harpe's read:

"John Setton who has been found guilty of robbery at the present term was this day set to the bar and the sentence of the court pronounced upon him as follows, that on Wednesday the eighth day of the present month he be taken to the place of execution and there to be hung up by the neck, between the hours of ten o'clock in the forenoon and four in the afternoon, until he is dead, dead, dead. Which said sentence the Sheriff of Jefferson County was ordered to carry into execution."

On the sunny afternoon of February 8, 1804, Harpe and Alston, under heavy guard, walked about a quarter of a mile north of Greenville.

There, before a sizable crowd, the Sheriff hung them. Thus, the two greedy murderers earned their just reward. It wasn't the reward they bargained for when they brought in Samuel Mason's head and tried to collect the $1,000 bounty on him.

The version of a hanging as shown in hundreds of movies was not how most pioneer executions took place in the late 17th and early 18th centuries. Occasionally, frontier executions included a well-constructed gallows complete with a trap door, but they were rare.

Usually, the court ordered executioner (commonly the county sheriff) built a makeshift gallows. He would fasten one end of a long beam, or heavy pole, in the fork of one tree, and the other end in the fork of another tree. A strong rope would be tied at the center of the beam, or pole. Generally the condemned prisoner, his hands bound, boarded a wagon, with his coffin serving as his seat. The sheriff drove the wagon to the place of execution. Once the wagon was beneath the rope, the sheriff would force the prisoner to stand erect atop the coffin, then loop the noose around the prisoner's neck. After reading the official pronouncement, and perhaps hearing a short prayer for the criminal's soul, the sheriff rushed the horses forward, causing them to pull the wagon from beneath the condemned prisoner, leaving him dangling above the ground. Since this type of hanging did not break the condemned criminal's neck, he choked and kicked, often for several minutes, until he asphyxiated.

The hanging of Harpe and Alston differed somewhat from typical frontier executions. In their case, the sheriff tied two ropes to a thick, heavy pole placed high between two trees. The two men didn't even get to ride to their demise. The sheriff prodded them along as they walked, their hands tied tightly behind them, from the jail to their gallows.

Then the sheriff forced each of them to mount a separate ladder. Once each prisoner was atop his ladder, he had his feet tied together and the noose fastened around his neck.

The men had the legal right to make a statement before the passing of the sentence upon them, and both took advantage of that. Of course, being the kind of men they were, neither expressed any remorse for their crimes.

Wiley "Redheaded" Harpe used his final words to try to extract revenge on some of his enemies. He confessed to several crimes, and then implicated a collection of people that, before then, were not under any suspicion of association with Samuel Mason or his gang.

When Alston's turn to speak came, he whimpered like the sniveling coward he was. He said he wasn't guilty of any crime deserving a noose. He then spoke of the service he had done for the community by "destroying old Mason." If Alston hoped to cause those hearing him to take pity on him and reconsider his sentence, he was mistaken. No one shed a tear for him.

After the two murderers finished speaking, the executioner pulled the ladders away and the two criminals dropped. There, suspended in midair, Harpe and Alston did the hangman's dance until they were, as the court ordered, "dead, dead, dead."

Simply following the legalities in the case in connection with Wiley Harpe and Peter Alston did not satisfy the community. The enraged townsfolk of Greenville believed these two outlaws deserved a fate worse than death for their crimes – known and unknown. A historian later wrote, "After their execution . . . their heads were placed on poles, one a short distance to the north and the other a short distance to the west of Greenville, on the Natchez Trace."

Perhaps it was fitting that Wiley Harpe suffered the same indignity after his death that his bloody brother received more than four years earlier.

It is impossible to say with any accuracy how long the disembodied heads stood along the road. But for the entire time their dead eyes stared across the trail, they stood as beacons of justice, warning other outlaws "the wages of sin is death."

After taking the heads as gruesome trophies, the scoundrels' remains needed disposal. The county coroner had the two bodies dumped into a single plain wooden box, and had the coffin buried late at night in a new graveyard about 100 yards east of the Greenville jail and courthouse. Fittingly, the graveyard was just beside the Natchez Trace, and mere feet from the pole on which hung one of the heads.

The burial of the headless outlaws caused controversy. Relatives of the half dozen or so persons already slumbering eternally in the cemetery complained bitterly that their loved ones would have to share a resting place with the two evil men. They attempted to convince county officials to bury the decapitated villains elsewhere. The officials declined the request and buried the bodies there anyway.

The lack of justice accorded their loved ones incensed those with relatives buried in the graveyard. The day after the box holding Harpe and Alston was buried, a number of indignant men exhumed it and carried it about a half mile south of Greenville, burying it in a place where no other body rested. Over time, other burials took place there, and it became known as the Bellegrove Church Yard.

Thus, the monstrous career of Wiley Harpe ended. America's first serial killers were finally dead, but the pain and horror the bloody brothers exacted from innocent men, women, and children lived on for decades afterward.

Afterword

CRIME on the Mississippi and along the Natchez Trace didn't end with the death of the notorious Harpe brothers. Even men of standing were not immune to the violence in that wild region. In 1809, famed explorer and Governor of Upper Louisiana Territory, Meriwether Lewis, died of gunshot wounds while traveling on Natchez Trace.

Over time, however, aided by America's acquisition of Louisiana, civilization took a better hold of the wilderness between the Smokey Mountains and the Mississippi River, and lawlessness declined. After the purchase of the vast area, outlaws had no safe place to nest west of the Mississippi, so had to look elsewhere to build their lairs. Of course, as pioneers pushed the edge of the frontier westerly, criminals moved along with the honest folk and remained a problem.

There is no ready answer as to why the Harpes became what they were. Many persons suffered through more than they did without becoming inhuman monsters. Even recent research by scientists of renown hasn't unraveled the dark mystery of serial killers. Perhaps there no explanation for the evil that walks among us. Regardless of why they exist, that serial murderers cause misery wherever they go is not in question.

After the atrocities committed by the Harpes became widely known, many of their family members changed their names to hide their heritage and separate themselves from their nefarious ancestors. This is understandable because on the frontier, memories were long and emotions remained high. Even distant relations of the Harpes had plenty to fear from those desiring retribution for the crimes of the bloody brothers.

When it came to the bloody brothers, retribution was impossible. How does shooting or hanging those evil beings recompense the scores of innocent men, women, and children they slaughtered? It doesn't.

Bibliography

Allen, William B. *A History of Kentucky, Embracing Gleanings, Reminiscences, Antiquities, Natural Curiosities, Statistics, and Biographical Sketches of Pioneers, Soldiers, Jurists, Lawyers, Statesmen, Divines, Mechanics, Farmers, Merchants, and other leading men* Louisville: Bradley & Gilbert, 1872.

Banta, R. E. *The Ohio*. Lexington, Kentucky: University Press of Kentucky, 1998.

Gammon, CL. *Bizarre Murders in Tennessee: 13 True Stories*. Lafayette, Tennessee: Createpace, 2013.

Gaylord, Charles. *The United States Criminal Calendar*. Boston, 1840.

George, Charles and Linda George. *The Natchez Trace*. New York: Children's Press, 2001.

Goode, Stephen. *Violence in America*. New York: Simon & Schuster, 1984.

Hall, James. *The Harpe's Head: A Legend of Kentucky*. New York: Key & Biddle, 1833.

Kahn, Joan, editor. *Some Things Dark and Dangerous*. New York: Harper and Row, 1970.

McQueen, Victor. *The World's Worst Psychopaths: The Most Depraved Killers in History*. London: Arcturus, 2015.

Mallet, Xanthe. "These are the Differences Between Psychopaths and Sociopaths." *Men's Health*, January 11, 2019.

Musgrave, Jon. "Frontier Serial Killers: The Harpes." *American Weekend*, October 23, 1998.

Newton, Michael, and John L. French. *Serial Killers*. New York: Chelsea House Publishers, 2008.

Ridley, Jim and Read Ridley. "Killing Cousins: The Terrifying True Story of the Harpes, who Terrorized Tennessee Two Centuries Ago – and Paid with Their Heads." *The Nashville Scene*, Oct 13, 2013.

Rosen, Fred. *The Historical Atlas of American Crime*. New York: Checkmark Books, 2005.

Rothert, Otto A. *A History of Muhlenberg County*. Louisville: John P. Morgan & Company, 1913.

Rothert, Otto A. *The Outlaws of CAVE-IN-ROCK*. Cleveland: Arthur H. Clark Company, 1924.

Schneider, Paul. *Old Man River: The Mississippi River in North American History*. New York: Macmillan, 2013.

Schram, Pamela, J. and Stephen G. Tibbetts. *Introduction to Criminology: Why Do They Do It?* Los Angeles: Sage, 2014.

Skowronek, Russell K. and Charles R. Ewen, editors. *X Marks the Spot: The Archaeology of Piracy*. Gainesville, Florida: University of Florida Press, 2007.

Smith, T. Marshall. *Legends of the War of Independence, and of the Earlier Settlements in the West*. Louisville: J. F. Brennan, 1855.

Stancil, Kristina. *North Mississippi Murder & Mayhem*. Charleston: The History Press, 2018.

Walters, Glenn D. *Foundations of Criminal Science. Vol. 1: The Development of Knowledge*. New York: Praeger Publishers, 1992.

About the Author

HENRY Lincoln Keel came to Kentucky from Germany in 1991. He has written extensively about 18th Century America.

Index

Alabama: 96

Allen, Ann L.: 136

Allen, John: 129

Alston, James, aka James May: 187, 199-204, 206-210, 212-214

Americans, Native: 15-16, 21, 83, 90, 93, 142, 144-145

Anthony, Abraham: 39

Appalachian Mountains: 15, 23

Arkansas: 5, 159-160, 164-165, 170, 209

Arkansas River: 148

Army, American: 11, 20, 131, 164-165, 179

Army, British: 12

Associators: 12

Atlantic Ocean: 15

Aycoff, Mr.: 26

Baker, Joshua: 150-154, 158, 169-170, 172, 176-178, 181-182

Baldwin, Mr.: 120

Ballard, William: 72-73, 79

Ballenger, Joseph: 40-41, 43, 52-54, 64

Barren River: 55, 61 63

Barret, Mr.: 173-174

Bass, Mr.: 146-147

Bassett, Mr.: 169, 176-177, 179

Bates, Mr.: 33-34

Battle of Blackstock's: 12

Battle of Blue Licks: 20

Battle of Cowpens: 12

Battle of Kings Mountain: 12, 95-96

Battle of the Bluffs: 20

Bear Creek: 155

Beaver Creek: 26

Bellegrove Churchyard: 214

Biegler, John: 44-45

Big Rock Castle River

Billeth, Pierre: 188-189

Black boy (murdered): 83

Black Oak Ridge: 71

Blair, John: 40, 48

Boone, Daniel: 20, 77, 90

Boone's Trace: 34

Bowman, John: 205

Bradbury, Mr.: 25

Bradbury Ridge: 25

Bradley, Captain: 188
Brassel, James: 72-75, 79
Brassel, Robert: 72-77
Brassel's Knob: 72
Breazeale and Parrot: 209-210
Briscoe, Philip: 173
Brown, Mr.: 173
Bruin, Peter, B.: 207
Burnett, Daniel: 153-154, 156
Burr, Aaron: 207
Burton, Mr.: 168
Butler, Anthony: 130-132
Campbell, Mr.: 169, 171
Canada: 144
Canoe Creek: 88-89, 92
Carolina, North: 5, 8-11, 19, 83, 147,
Carolina, South, Charleston: 81
Caston, Seth: 207
Cave-In-Rock: 51, 64, 66-69, 71, 78, 80, 143, 157, 182, 197, 206
Cherokees: 20-21, 83-84
Choctaws: 146, 164, 177
Choctaw Trace: 196
Christian, Matthew: 105-106, 108, 114-118, 126, 134-135, 137

Claiborne, William: 148-150, 152-156, 159, 193-194, 202, 205
Clinch River: 29
Coffey, Chesley (son murdered): 71-73, 79
Cole's Creek: 196-197
Colin, Charles: 168
Concer, Felic: 185
Cumberland Gap: 32, 35
Cumberland Mountains; 29
Cumberland River: 34, 144, 166, 189
Dale, Mr.: 74-76
Dearborn, James: 156
Deer Creek: 93, 123
Derousser, Francois: 187-188
Devil, The: 17, 25
Diamond Island: 64-67, 143
Dooley, Mr.: 61
Doss, Moses: 20
Douglas, Marguerite: 174, 183-184
Downs, James: 189
Downs, William: 170, 172, 178-179, 182, 208
Dragging Canoe, Chief: 20
Duck River: 131
Duff brothers: 182
Dunlap, Hugh: 72

Ellis, John: 79-80
Emery River: 72
English's Ferry: 35
Farris, Jane: 36-38, 43
Farris, John, Sr.: 35-36, 38-39, 43
Ferris, William: 43
Ferguson, Patrick: 12
Fort Gibson: 152-200
Fort Henry: 142
Fort Pickering: 148
France: 144, 162
Free Henry Ford: 113
Fulsom, Mr.: 165, 169, 176-177, 180
Galley, *Louisiana*: 164
Garrard, James: 52, 57-58, 61, 65, 79
Georgia: 26
Geyon's Corps: 164
Gibson, Mr.: 165
Glass, Anthony: 169, 171-172, 179
Graves, John (and son): 82
Great Smokey Mountains: 19, 215
Green River, aka "Rouge's Harbor"): 51, 63-64, 66, 83, 183
Grindstone Ford: 154
Grissom, William: 104-106, 108, 114-116, 134-135
Grundy, Felix: 129

Hardin, Mr.: 79
Harpe, Betsey: 19, 42, 46-48, 127, 130-131
Harpe, Lovey: 131-132
Harpe, Micajah: (Early Days: 8-10); (During the Revolution: 11-13); (In Tennessee: 14-18); (With the Renegades: 19-22); (After Nickajack: 23-29); (A trail of blood: 30-39); (Escape form justice: 40-45); (At Cave-In-Rock: 51-70); (More murders: 71-87); (Capture and death: 88-124)
Harpe, Sarah, aka Sally: 26, 42, 46-48, 109-110, 112-114, 127, 131-133
Harpe, Susan, aka Susana: 12, 19, 37, 42, 46-48, 86-87, 97-98, 118, 122, 127, 129, 131-132
Harpe, Wiley: (Early Days: 8-10); (During the Revolution: 11-13); (In Tennessee: 14-18); (With the Renegades: 19-22); (After Nickajack: 23-29); (A trail of blood: 30-39); (Escape form justice: 40-45); (At Cave-In-Rock: 51-70); (More murders: 71-87); (Rejoining Mason: 141-160); (Testimony: 161-190); (Another escape:

191-195); (Capture and death: 196-214)

Harpe's Head Road: 123

Harper, Joshua: 9

Harper, William: 9

Highland Creek: 88, 91

Holstein River: 30

Hopkins, Samuel: 79, 92, 125-126

Hudgens, Mr., (murder of): 102-103, 107

Hufstetter, John: 130-131

Hughes Rowdy Groggery: 30-32

Hughes, Mr.: 30-32

Hunter, James G.: 47, 129

Huston, Nathan: 42

Illinois: 5, 64-65, 70, 126, 133, 135, 144, 155, 182, 187

Indiana: 126

Irby, David: 34-35, 39, 43

Johnson, Mr.: 30-32

Jones, Rees: 189

Kaskaskia Island: 189

Kentucky: 5, 20, 32-35, 42, 44, 46, 49, 52-53, 57, 61-62, 65, 70, 76, 78, 80-81, 83, 90, 92, 125-126, 129, 134, 139, 141, 144, 150, 152, 171, 183, 185-186, 205-206, 209; (Adair County: 136); (Adairville 83); (Bowling Green: 61); (Caldwell County: 120); (Carpenter's Station: 40); (Christian County: 103, 132); (Columbia: 54-55); (Danville: 44, 47-50, 52, 57-58, 63, 66, 205); (Dixon: 97, 123); (Eddyville 123); (Edmonton) 61; (Frankfort: 34-35, 40, 58, 79, 81); (Green County: 78); (Green Tree Grove: 120); (Henderson, aka Red Banks: 63-64, 66-67, 79-81, 123, 143, 184-185, 187-188); (Henderson County: 65. 67. 88-90, 125-126, 135-136, 197, 206); (Hustonville: 40); (Lincoln County: 33, 40, 42, 44, 46-47, 52); (Logan County: 39, 41-42, 48, 83-84, 127); (Louisville, aka Falls of the Ohio: 184, 186); (Madison: 123); (Mammoth Cave: 83); (Marion: 123); (Mercer County: 52, 64-65); (Metcalf County: 61); (Muhlenberg County: 121); (Orchard Crab: 33-35, 40, 50); (Russell County: 82); (Russellville: 83, 85, 88, 123, 126, 128, 131-132); (Sebree: 89); (Smithland: 69); (Stanford: 33, 40-41, 44); (Webster County: 89)

Ker, David: 207

Knob Lick: 88

Knox, James: 53

Koiret, Mr.: 168-169

Lafond, Charles: 184-185, 188

Lake Concordia: 201

Lake Providence: 158

Landers, Abraham: 125

Langford, Stephen: 34-43, 45, 47-49, 52

Lecompte, Mr.: 182

Leiper, John: 105-106, 108, 114-117, 126, 134-137, 139

Lewis, Meriwether: 215

Lindsay, Neville: 106, 108, 118, 121, 135

Little Girl (murdered): 82

Logan, Hugh: 42

Louisiana: 5, 70, 143-144, 149, 158-159, 162-163, 191, 193, 196, 201, 204, 209, 215; (New Orleans: 149-151, 155, 164, 184-185, 188-191, 193-194, 199); (Pointe Coupee: 194)

Louisiana Purchase: 144, 204, 215

Love, William: 98-101, 105, 110, 122, 126

Madison, James: 156

Magby, Silas: 105-106

Manuel, Father: 182, 189

Marrowbone Creek: 81

Maryland: 33-34, 38, 51

Mason Gang: 67, 141, 143-145, 148, 150-151, 156-161, 163-167, 170-171, 176-177, 189, 196-200, 203, 206, 212

Mason, John: 169-170, 172, 174-178, 180-182, 185

Mason, Magnus: 183-184

Mason, Mother: 167, 185, 202

Mason Samuel, Sr.: 67, 70, 141-146, 148, 150-159, 161-164, 166-168, 170-204, 206, 209, 211-212

Mason, Samuel, Jr.: 183

Mason, Thomas: 165, 167, 170, 172, 174-177, 180-182, 185-186

McBee Silas: 95-97, 101-114, 118-122, 134-135, 141, 146, 155

McCoy, Robert: 190-195, 197, 201

McDowell, Samuel: 47, 129

McFarland, Alexander: 65, 134

McFarland, Daniel: 65, 134

McFarland, John: 65, 134

McGee, John: 85

McGee, William: 85

McGready, James: 85
Metcalf brothers: 30-32
Miller, John: 27
Mississippi: 5, 88, 96, 146, 149, 155, 157, 163, 196, 202, 206-209; (Bayou Pierre: 183-184, 199); (Claiborne County: 153); (Fayette: 158); (Greenville: 197-199, 207, 210, 213-214); (Hinds County: 151); (Jackson: 151); (Jefferson County: 196, 201, 207, 210); (Natchez: 144, 149, 154-155, 158, 161, 171, 176, 182-184, 194-197, 199-200, 202, 204-205, 207); (Pearl: 132); (Pontotoc: 135); (Rocky Springs: 158); (Rodney: 201); (Vicksburg: 152, 158, 164, 168, 170-171, 178, 181, 183); (Walnut Hills: 152-154); (Washington: 152); (Yazoo: 154)
Mississippi Militia; 153-154, 158-159, 190, 196, 200
Mississippi River: 15, 70, 144-145, 148-150, 152-153, 155-156, 158-159, 161-162, 165, 168, 170, 189, 191, 193, 196-198, 215
Missouri: (Little Prairie, now Caruthersville: 161, 165, 168, 178, 197); (New Madrid: 144-145, 161, 163, 184-185, 187-189, 191, 193, 195); (St. Genevieve: 189); (St. Louis: 182)
Montgomery, William: 42
Morgantown Road: 85
Mosique, Mr.: 182
Mud River: 85
Natchez Trace: 144-146, 148, 152, 154, 158, 161, 168, 170, 197, 204, 213-215
Nicholson, William: 172
Ohio, Cincinnati: 81
Ohio River: 63-69, 91, 133, 135, 139, 143-145, 184-187, 189
Ohio Valley: 64, 66
Ormsby, Stephen: 47
Overmountain Men: 12
Owsley, Mr.: 169-171, 175-176, 178-179, 181
Paca, Mr.: 33-34
Peltier, Eustache: 188
Pennsylvania: 143, 165, 183
Peyton, Mr.: 33
Phillips, Mr.: 169, 171, 176, 180
Poindexter, Mr.: 208-209
Pond River: 107, 111, 118-119, 132
Powell's Valley: 23
Pyles, John: 103-104
Rape Gang: 11-12, 21

Red River: 131
Regulator War: 9
Regulators: 32
Rennick, Seymour: 154
Revolutionary War: 9, 11-13, 20, 54, 59, 93, 95, 125, 142, 144, 173
Rice John: 26, 133
Roberts, "Old Man": 82-83, 136
Roberts, Joe: 131
Robertson, Robert: 137
Robertson's Lick: 88, 90-91, 102-105, 122-123
Rodney, Thomas: 207
Rolling Fork: 53
Salcedo, Manuel de: 149-150, 189, 193-194
Saline River: 64
Salt River: 53
Scotland: 8-9
Sellers, Isom: 97-98, 126
Seneca Tribe: 143
Skaggs, Henry: 53-57
Slave(s): 10, 13, 59, 83, 107, 142, 147, 182, 187, 189
Smith, Druck, aka Smith Gibson: 165, 169, 176, 180, 185
Smith, George: 110-112
Slover, John: 90-92
Spain: 144, 162
Spain, King of: 164

Sparks, Richard: 148
Spears, George: 55
St. Francis River: 165
Stack Island: 158
Stegall, James: 100-102, 126
Stegall, Mary: 98-102, 126
Stegall, Moses: 97-98, 101, 103-106, 108, 111, 114-116, 119-123, 126, 128-129, 134-140
Steuben Lick: 93
Steuben, Friedrich Wilhelm von: 93
Stewart, William: 84, 127-130, 133
Stockton, Nathaniel: 77-79
Strong, W. E.: 52
Stump, Frederick: 204-205
Stump, Mr. (murder): 61-63
Tarleton, Banastre: 12
Tennessee: 5, 14, 20, 32, 35, 50, 52. 55, 57, 71, 76, 80-81, 84, 88, 129-131, 135, 145, 147, 153, 206, 209; (Chattanooga: 20); (Harriman Junction: 72); (Hawkins County: 147); (Jefferson County: 30); (Knox County: 33, 98); (Knoxville: 23, 25-30, 49-51, 65, 71-75, 79, 130, 133, 138, 155, 205); (Memphis, "Chickasaw Bluff": 148); (Morgan

County: 72); (Nashville, "Fort Nashborough," "Bluff Station": 20, 144, 146); (Nickajack: 20-23); (Pickett County: 76); (Roane County: 71); (Williamson County: 146)

Tennessee River: 144, 155

Texas: 132

Tiel, Edward: 28-31

Todd, Thomas: 45

Tompkins, James: 93-95, 97, 106, 108, 114-115, 188, 121, 134-135

Toulmin, Harry: 58

Trabue, Daniel: 54, 56, 78-81, 136

Trabue, John: 55-57, 78, 136

Trade Water River: 139

Triswold brothers: 84

Trowbridge, Mr.: 91

Tucker, Sarah McBee: 96

Tucker, Tilghman Mayfield: 96

Tully, Christiana: 79

Tully, John: 76-79

Unity Baptist Church: 117

Vidal, Louisiana Secretary of War: 193

Virginia Militia: 142

Virginia: 10, 32, 35, 38, 42, 125, 144; (Norfolk: 142); (Mecklenburg County: 34); (Pittsylvania County: 34); (Wythe County: 35)

Wales, Dr.: 174

Washington, George: 11, 24, 125

Waters, Dr. Richard Jones: 184-186

Weir, James: 25

Welsh Joseph: 44, 52

Welsh, Thomas: 43

West Virginia, Charles Town: 142

White River: 159-160, 165

White, Robert: 134

Wiguens, Mr.: 165, 169, 176-177

Wilderness Road: 33-34, 36

Williams, Thomas Hill: 96

Winters, Elisha: 199, 210

Wood, Frank: 12

Wood, James: 11-12, 19, 82

Wood, William: 77-79

Young, Captain: 64-65, 67, 70, 89, 170

www.ingramcontent.com/pod-product-compliance
Lightning Source LLC
Chambersburg PA
CBHW061638040426
42446CB00010B/1484